# PUMPKINFLOWERS

ALSO BY MATTI FRIEDMAN

*The Aleppo Codex: In Pursuit of One of the World's*
*Most Coveted, Sacred, and Mysterious Books*

# Pumpkinflowers

AN ISRAELI SOLDIER'S STORY

## Matti Friedman

SIGNAL

McCLELLAND
& STEWART

Signal is an imprint of McClelland & Stewart, a division of
Penguin Random House Canada Limited, a Penguin Random House Company

Signal and colophon are registered trademarks of McClelland & Stewart,
a division of Penguin Random House Canada Limited, a Penguin Random House Company

**Library and Archives Canada Cataloguing in Publication**

Friedman, Matti, author
Pumpkinflowers : an Israeli soldiers story / Matti Friedman.
Issued in print and electronic formats.
ISBN 978-0-7710-3690-3 (bound). —ISBN 978-0-7710-3691-0 (epub)
1. Friedman, Matti.  2. Lebanon—History—Civil War, 1975-1990--
Personal narratives, Israeli.  I. Title.
DS87.5.F75 2016          956.9204'4          C2015-907752-4
                                             C2015-907753-2

The excerpt from John Prine's "Angel from Montgomery"
appears here with the permission of Alfred Music.

The permission to include part of Be'eri Hazak's poem
"Lord of the Universe" was granted by the author's brother, the poet
Yehiel Hazak. Translation by the author.

Text design by Steve Godwin
Jacket design by High Design
Jacket photo © AP Photo / Ariel Schalit
Printed and bound in the United States of America

McClelland & Stewart,
a division of Penguin Random House Canada Limited,
a Penguin Random House Company
www.penguinrandomhouse.ca

1  2  3  4  5      20  19  18  17  16

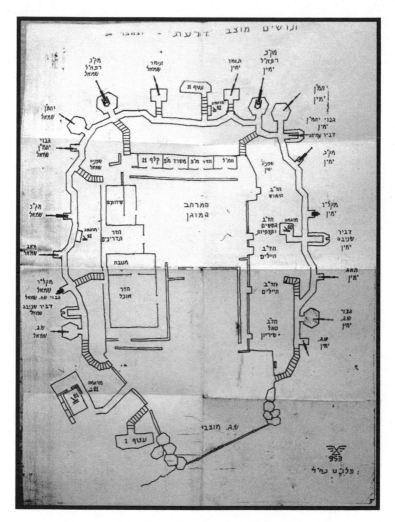

*A map of the Pumpkin distributed to soldiers (1998)*

**N**IGHTS ON THE hill were unusually long. They were inhabited by shadows flitting among boulders, by bushes that assumed human form, by viscous mists that crept in and thickened until all the sentries were blind. Sometimes you took over one of the guard posts, checked your watch an hour later, and found that five minutes had passed.

The enemy specialized in the roadside bomb artfully concealed, in the short barrage, in the rocket threaded through the slit of a guard post. We specialized in waiting. An honest history of this time would consist of several thousand pages of daydreams and disjointed thoughts born of exhaustion and boredom, disrupted only every hundred pages or so by a quick tragedy, and then more waiting.

At night four sentries waited in four guard posts that were never empty. Four crewmen waited in a tank, searching the approaches to the fort. Ambush teams conversed in whispers and passed cookies around in the undergrowth outside, waiting for guerrillas. A pair of soldiers drank coffee from plastic cups in a room of radio sets, waiting for transmissions to come through.

Before the earliest hint of dawn each day someone went around rousing all of those who weren't awake already. Groggy creatures dropped from triple-decker bunks, struggled into their gear, and snapped helmet straps under chins. Now everyone was supposed to be ready. Lebanon was dark at first, but soon the sky began to pale through the camouflage net. Sometimes first light would reveal that the river valley had filled with clouds, and then the Pumpkin felt like an island fortress in a sea of mist—like the only place in the world, or like a place not of this world at all. There was a mood of purposefulness at that hour, an intensity of connection among us, a kind of inaudible hum that I now understand was the possibility of death; it was exciting, and part of my brain misses it though other parts know better.

This ritual, the opening act of every day, might have been called Morning Alert or some other forgettable military term, with any unnecessary syllable excised. It might have been shortened, as so much of our language was, to an acronym. But for some reason it was never called anything but Readiness with Dawn. The phrase is as strange in the original Hebrew as in the English. This was, in our grim surroundings, a reminder that things need not be merely utilitarian. It was an example of the poetry that you can find even in an army, if you're looking.

The hour of Readiness with Dawn was intended as an antidote to the inevitable relaxing of our senses, a way of whetting the garrison's dulled attention as the day began. It was said this was the guerrillas' preferred time to storm the outpost, but they didn't do that when I was there. I remember standing in the trench as the curtain rose on our surroundings, trying to remember that out there, invisible, was the enemy, but finding my thoughts wandering instead to the landscape materializing at that moment beyond the coils of wire: cliffs and grassy slopes, villages balanced on the sides of mountains, a river flowing beneath us toward the Mediterranean. Things were so quiet that I believe I could hear the hill talking to me. I'm not sure I could understand then what it was saying. But now I believe it was "What are you doing here?" And also "Why don't you go home?"

That hill is still speaking to me years later. Its voice, to my surprise, has not diminished with the passage of time but has grown louder and more distinct.

This book is about the lives of young people who finished high school and then found themselves in a war—in a forgotten little corner of a forgotten little war, but one that has nonetheless reverberated in our lives and in the life of our country and the world since it ended one night in the first spring of the new century. Anyone looking for the origins of the Middle East of today would do well to look closely at these events.

Part 1 is about a series of incidents beginning in 1994 at the Israeli army outpost we called the Pumpkin, seen through the eyes of a soldier, Avi, who was there before me. Part 2 introduces two civilians, mothers, who helped bring about the unraveling of the military's strategy. Part 3 describes my own time on the hill, and the experiences of several of my friends in the outpost's last days. The final part recounts my return to Lebanon after these events had ended, in an attempt to understand them better.

Readiness with Dawn ended up being a time for contemplation.

Look around: Where are you, and why? Who else is here? Are you ready? Ready for what? So important was this ritual at such an important time in my life that this mode of consciousness became an instinct, the way an infant knows to hold its breath underwater. I still slip into it often. I'm there now.

# PUMPKINFLOWERS

# Part One

# 1

AT AN ENCAMPMENT imposed upon the sand near an empty highway, teenagers lined up in a yard. There were perhaps three hundred
of them, and in their floppy sunhats they looked like comical green
mushrooms sprouting in rows from the tarmac. The conventions of
military writing seem to require that they be described from now on
as "men." But this would hardly have applied a few days earlier.

Someone read from a list, and two dozen strangers whose names
were called became a platoon of engineers. This, at least, was how one
of the military clerks might have explained what had just happened.
What had in fact been determined was the course—and, in a few
cases, the duration—of their lives. What led them here? The shuffling
of forms in distant offices, the nature of their upbringing and youth-
ful motivations, the astonishing progression of their people's history
in the century approaching its end. It didn't matter now. Some would
break and vanish in the coming months, but the rest—from now on
their fates were welded to one another and to the hilltop at the center
of this story. It was early in the spring of 1994. *Do you have to, do you
have to, do you have to let it linger . . .* You remember.

Avi was another figure in a row: shorter than most, more solid than most, a combative black-eyed flash suggesting he was less obedient than most. What was he doing among the others? He disliked authority and it was mutual, the nature of their relationship traceable to an incident a decade earlier. He and his classmates were to give a little bow during a visit by the president of Israel, Avi refused, his parents were summoned, and he said, I will not bow down. Perhaps he had been paying overly close attention to a book; the incident sounds like it may have been inspired by the character of Mordechai from the book of Esther. He was six or seven at the time.

This sort of thing recurred in subsequent years. He was supposed to be studying in the months leading up to the date of his draft, but one day when he should have been in class his parents found him instead sitting outside with a cigarette in one hand and, in the other, *Zen and the Art of Motorcycle Maintenance*. He became an individual early. Long before he turned eighteen and was summoned to his three years of military service, he had developed the habit of standing to one side and watching everyone, including himself. Much later some of Avi's friends were able to see what happened to them in those years in the army from a distance, and they grasped their own place in the confusing sweep of events, but none had that ability at the time. Avi did. It didn't make things easier for him.

I didn't know Avi then and might not have liked him if I had. I felt fortunate to discover him now—not only because he experienced many of the incidents that will concern us here, and not only because he is a good example of the kind of person changed or ground up by war, but because I have met enough people by now to know you don't find someone like him often.

Avi was suspicious of institutions like the military, and his experiences would confirm that these suspicions were justified. He had already decided that he scorned hierarchies and official ideology. He once announced that he was going to move to Ireland one day, and it wasn't clear if he was joking. But he wasn't a shirker. So he stood in a yard that day in unfamiliar clothes, surrounded by unfamiliar faces, and heard his name called.

# 2

OBSERVING AVI AND the other recruits two decades later, you can see they were on the cusp of something. They were eyeing adulthood and wondering what it would mean, just as now they do the same with middle age, those who are still here. But it wasn't just that. They wrote letters, as we'll see. They had no electronic communication devices. Their world seems so quiet. The army was still very much the old army with old ideas about war, but the war for which Avi was bound was different and augured others to come. The world that day at the desert base was, in other words, the past. For the men selected along with Avi, and for many others, what marks the line between the past and the present, between youth and everything that has happened since, is the hill in Lebanon that we called the Pumpkin.

From the first moment everything was pulling them away from the deserts of Israel's south to the country's northern edge, toward the border with Lebanon and then across. The desert plays here only the role usually allotted it in the ancient stories about this country—an in-between land, a space for preparation.

# 3

THE ARMY REPLACED the trappings of Avi's former life—jeans, books, sandals, T-shirts with the neck cut off in the Israeli style of those years—with new objects. These included a rifle; boots of stiff red leather; fatigues distributed in unpredictable sizes by harried quartermasters; crates of sharp, glinting golden baubles that were heaped like pirate doubloons but were 5.56 mm bullets. His parents were replaced by sergeants and officers.

The commanders at the desert base had to teach these kids to obey orders, fire their rifles, walk long distances with heavy packs, and then, at the point of collapse, to run. They needed to replace opinions with instincts and demonstrate that physical limits are a matter of will. When the kids failed they needed to be punished by the imposition of a distance to sprint in an impossibly short time and then, having failed to achieve that, made to sprint again and again, not until they succeeded—they could not—but until the grins of the cockier ones slackened and the weaker ones began to sniffle. Medics needed to learn to apply a tourniquet and get an intravenous needle in someone's arm in the dark, machine gunners to clear a jammed weapon. Radiomen needed to learn the language spoken on the Israeli military frequencies: bullets are "candies," food is "hot and tasty," soldiers are "matches." The fresh eyes of the recruits needed to be dulled into a haggard stare. Their faces needed to lose the softness of childhood and assume, via some alchemy of sunburn, sweat, and responsibility, the definition of adults.

Avi and the others belonged to an infantry brigade with a lovely relic of a name: the Fighting Pioneer Youth. This was not an outfit with any particular reputation for valor in battle. It was famous largely for having a first-rate entertainment troupe in the 1960s, when the army was still investing in song-and-dance routines and comedy sketches. By the time Avi arrived the Fighting Pioneer Youth Entertainment Troupe was a thing of the past, but its hits were classics, and its enduring fame had the effect of making the brigade of that name seem less serious than others.

The Fighting Pioneer Youth tended to be youth who understood that combat service was necessary but were by no means pioneers or enamored with the idea of fighting. The brigade had no warlike slogans or symbols; for an infantry unit, it was unusually humane. The idea was not "death before dishonor," "no surrender," or anything like that but rather "let's get through this."

Avi got used to sleeping on a cot with other soldiers inches from him on either side, his rifle underneath his head, the thin green mattress keeping his cheek from the cold metal of the gun. The recruits were soon too tired to notice the discomfort, or to dream.

# 4

"A. REACHED BASIC training young, healthy, and innocent." This is Avi, writing of himself in the third person.

When the sergeant said to do things on time he did, and when the commander ordered everyone to give him 50 push-ups A. was the one who set the pace.

But the danger of innocence is that it gets cracked easily by stupidity and cruelty. And so not much time had passed before A. started thinking that perhaps it was not right that he was the only one who was not late, or that he was the only one who cared when the sergeant threw him a good word. His concern grew when he heard the other members of the platoon saying that the regular punishments of running back and forth were not even punishments for something they had done wrong! They were, instead, a plot by the sergeants—that is, the system—directed against them! A. began thinking about this until he could no longer sleep during the short nights allotted to them. He thought so much that he began to move slowly in the morning himself, and to run slowly when they were punished. Because all of his faculties were devoted to the problem, he did not notice anything else, and quickly became the slowest and deafest of soldiers. Because one of the commanders would speak to him on occasion and interrupt his thoughts, A. suddenly understood that what they wanted to do was prevent him from thinking. He understood that they were his real enemies! They were the enemies of thought and creativity who wanted to enslave him and turn him into a creature incapable of thought, and willing to obey them.

This thought scared him so badly that he began resisting in any way he could. He started to think and do things his own way. If they gave him a mission, like setting the tables in the dining hall, he would put the cutlery backwards! Or miss on purpose at the firing range!! Now he was a rebel!!! And thus A. fought the system, and to the best of our knowledge he might still be doing so today, somewhere in the time and space of the army . . .

Avi was a difficult recruit. He was also a writer—not a great one yet, but on his way.

# 5

A FEW MONTHS passed in the desert.

Avi and his comrades camped in a cluster of pup tents several miles from the base. By this time they had been assigned roles and gear, and Avi had a black tube attached to the bottom of his rifle that fired fist-sized grenades in shiny yellows and greens. The rifle was too long for his body, and he resented its weight. Their faces were sunburned, the skin of their knuckles cracked and chafed, their knees gashed by the vicious little stones that cover the training grounds in that part of the Negev. Their fatigues showed black smears of gun grease and white circles left behind by dried sweat. A minute's walk away from camp took them to the toilet paper scraps and sun-dried shit of their improvised latrine.

They were now accustomed to suffering. When soldiers are glimpsed in the real world outside the army they tend to be looking their best, which can be misleading, because out of sight in their own world their existence is miserable. You are always looking for a way to keep warm, for something to eat, or a place to lie down. You are grimy, and depleted, and your life is not your own, and you are pushed at times to levels of despondence and desperation that are quite extreme. You find yourself in the company of your friends not marching proudly or even sprinting bravely, as you might have thought, but rather, in Wilfred Owen's words, "bent double, like old beggars under sacks." To be an infantryman is to experience a kind of poverty. This is one of the things that make it worthwhile, but only in retrospect.

The specialized companies of the Fighting Pioneer Youth attract an unusual crowd, one more intellectual than the average infantry draft, but this was an unusual platoon even by those standards. Take Matan, one of Avi's new friends: Matan had found little to stimulate his mind on his kibbutz and claimed not to have read a book of his own volition since *Where Is Pluto?*, a picture book about a dog who goes for a walk and falls into a pond. But now he discovered that among his comrades were people who thought and read and were still doing so, somehow, under the oppressive conditions of basic training. When his tent mate, Amos, brought a book of philosophical meditations called *In the Footsteps of Thoughts* he and Matan actually read it and then talked about it for weeks, lying sore on the ground after days of exertion, breathing the smell of their own unwashed bodies, of earth, and of dusty canvas. It was an assertion of the freedom of their minds. Matan thought at first that they would be mocked. But though the others sometimes yelled at them to shut up and go to sleep, no one laughed. Today Matan is a physicist. Amos is a psychiatrist and lives in Paris.

Avi made a point of saying exactly what he thought, and a few of the soldiers suffered from the acidity of his commentary, typically delivered without regard for the feelings of others. One of them, Ilya, remembers that Avi made it clear from the beginning that he considered Ilya to be dim-witted, revising his opinion only when he learned that Ilya had read *One Hundred Years of Solitude*. Avi was never considered a leader in the platoon. But his presence was very much felt, and not always welcome, certainly not at first. Photographs of this time show Avi with the expression of a kid emerging into a world he was not sure he would like, or would like him.

Basic training is like marriage: inside its unforgiving intimacy you can't hide who you are for long. Soon Avi softened. It turned out that he always had books in his knapsack, and when he saw he wasn't alone he began passing them around.

One picture of Avi as a child shows him asleep on his bed surrounded by books and newspapers, and another, taken a few years later, shows him sitting on one side of a room reading at his own birthday party. In high school the librarian, making her rounds at the end of the day, used to find him sitting on a footstool by one of the windows, immobilized by a volume plucked from the shelf: *Brideshead Revisited*, *Murder on the Orient Express*, Nevil Shute's *Pied Piper*. He grew up rooted in the small country where he was born, to lullabies like the famous one Emmanuel the Russian wrote in the 1920s:

Here you will sprout, here you will grow
In the land of Israel
To happiness, to labor
Like your father, you will be a worker.
Then you will sow in tears
And reap with joy
But now listen to *Ima*
Please sleep

By high school, as his reading list shows, he was looking for glimpses of other places. When the army called him, his favorite literary guide to the world was Romain Gary, immigrant outsider turned hero of the Free French Air Force; France's consul-general to Hollywood; husband of the actress Jean Seberg and lover of countless others, beginning, if his own account is to be believed, with the maid at age thirteen; Mallorca hedonist; two-time winner of the Prix Goncourt (a feat not technically possible and never repeated), each time under a different name, neither of them his own; child of the same inflamed European Jewish world that yielded Isaac Bashevis Singer, Vasily Grossman, Leonard Cohen, Avi's grandparents, and the state of Israel itself.

Avi conducted a survey. Who had read Gary's masterpiece *The Kites*, an account of a love affair in Normandy under Nazi rule between the daughter of a Polish count and the peasant nephew of an eccentric kite maker? No one? Avi circulated his paperback copy, which was shoved into webbing pouches and nestled in packs among filthy socks. It is possible to imagine that Gary, the shape-shifter of Vilna and Nice, was thus present among them somehow, that in one of their two-man pup tents there was an invisible third occupant with a Gauloise and an empathetic smile.

# 6

DURING THE LAST weeks of training the members of Avi's platoon discovered a common language and each found his own place in their tiny social world. This sometimes happens in a small unit, if you're lucky. Friendship in a platoon is created under great pressure and is difficult to explain to those who have not experienced it themselves; armies plan it this way, knowing the strength of this bond is what will keep men together and functioning in the lawless netherworld of war and, when the time comes, cause them to commit the unreasonable act of following each other not away from enemy fire but into it.

It began to seem as if someone had chosen most members of this particular platoon not for their physical abilities or soldierly potential but for their intelligence and disposition, and specifically a cynicism about the military itself. This seems unlikely but isn't impossible. They had all been interviewed before the lists were drawn up at the training base, and whoever was in charge of selecting the soldiers for the brigade's engineering company might simply have chosen the ones he liked. That officer was perhaps the person with the greatest impact on the lives of the members of Avi's platoon, his invisible stamp on everything that has happened to them since, but when I sat with them recently in Avi's parents' living room—they are nearly forty now and still have an easy way with each other all these years later—no one remembered a thing about him.

An unspoken agreement formed in the platoon: they were in this for each other, not for the army. Sergeants, officers, and clerks were to be despised and resisted. One of the countless rules governing the recruits' lives banned eating when posted to guard the gate of the base. But early in basic training Avi looked around, confirmed that he was unobserved, and pulled out a bag of chocolate pastries, ammunition in his fight against the system. What united the members of the platoon was "an ironic half step of distance from what was happening to us"—this is how Amos, the psychiatrist, remembers it. There is a rhetorical question in common usage in our military for motivational purposes: "If things get a little hard, you give up?" This is supposed to shame you into pushing forward when you can no longer move your legs. Avi's platoon celebrated this as their philosophy after making a small change to the punctuation: If things get a little hard, you give up.

Beneath this outward language of rebellion was the fact, usually unspoken, that they didn't have to be here. If you didn't want to be a combat soldier you could get out of it, and no one had to volunteer for the more rigorous training and dangerous service of the engineers. Their presence meant that however they regarded this callous organization, the army, they understood that the threats facing their country were real and that this demand of them was legitimate. Your turn comes. They wouldn't have said it themselves because of a social code mandating self-deprecation and sarcasm and forbidding any credulous expression of ideals, so it needs to be said on their behalf: they believed they were doing the right thing.

They listened to Springsteen, especially "The River," and to the Cranberries. They gave each other nicknames. Gal, a quiet boy who became one of Avi's closest friends, was "the Angel," because he always found time to help others. Avi was known as "the Skunk." While it is unclear now precisely what led to this choice, if you've been an eighteen-year-old male among eighteen-year-old males it is possible to guess. The Angel and the Skunk were an odd pair—one tall and gentle, the other small and easily bruised or provoked.

The sergeants sent Avi and his fellow philosophers and dissidents running up hills to shoot at cardboard cutouts of enemy soldiers and then made them do it again. They oversaw drills on the firing range: five bullets standing, five kneeling, five prone. The recruits became accustomed to the rifle's kick and the sharp smell of cordite. Avi ran the obstacle course, which meant climbing a rope in full gear, crawling on his stomach, and getting over a shoulder-high concrete wall; the latter was the nemesis of many recruits, its malevolent blank grayness a feature of nightmares. The sergeants had them eighteen hours on their feet, six hours in their sleeping bags, then up again in the dark and off into the hills.

It shouldn't surprise anyone familiar with military thinking that Avi's platoon spent a great deal of time training not for the guerrilla war that actually awaited them but instead to open a minefield for the passage of immense formations of infantry and tanks and to conquer desert hills—to fight what the army saw as the "real war," one that fit its pretensions more than inconclusive skirmishing in Lebanese bushes. It was 1994, but the army's clock was still set at 1973. This certainly wouldn't have surprised Avi's beloved Romain Gary, who found himself as an air force cadet communicating with hand signals from the open cockpit of a Potez 25 biplane going seventy miles per hour, being "actively trained, like the French Army, for the war of 1914" in 1938.

In the years of these events, the 1990s, many people in Israel thought peace was coming, and if you look through old newspapers you'll find lots of news about peace negotiations. People were talking at the time about a "new Middle East," and the war in Lebanon was of less interest. So civilians in Israel were thinking about this new Middle East, and the army about the real war, but nothing came of either—it turned out that what was happening in Lebanon was both the new Middle East and the new real war. Something important was afoot while everyone looked elsewhere, and marginal events turned out to be the ones of most significance. This is often the case.

It was at around this time that Avi began hearing about the assignment awaiting them once training was over. No one knew much yet, just that it was a hill in Lebanon.

At the end of October 1994, a few weeks before they were scheduled to board a convoy for the hill, the Pumpkin Incident occurred. The current garrison needed to be relieved early. Avi and his friends were ordered to pack and head north.

# 7

ISRAELI COMBAT TROOPS in those days were divided into those who had been in Lebanon and those who had not. Among those who had, the question was how far inside you had been and what perils you had faced. If you fell behind in a training march as a recruit, the sergeants would say: Who'll push you forward in Lebanon? If you struggled to operate the radio on your back while lying prostrate on the ground, they rocketed stones off your helmet and asked: Who'll help you in Lebanon? The answer was no one. The point was that you couldn't fail. If you did, you would be one of those guys who smiled at newspaper readers every few weeks.

My intention here is not to get bogged down in historical explanation. I would rather suggest the title of a comprehensive history of these years of the Lebanon "security zone" in the 1990s, for those interested in background, and continue Avi's story uninterrupted; unfortunately no such history has been written. These events were important when they were going on, and left intense personal memories. But they left barely any collective memory at all. What remain are a few dramatic incidents vaguely recalled, related to each other in ways no longer entirely clear. The period doesn't even have a name.

Though hardly distant, it is already sinking into the depths behind us, soon to be unrecoverable. So a few words are necessary about the series of events into which the rebel A. is about to be inserted.

Southern Lebanon in the nineties evoked something of Spain in the thirties, the scene of violent jostling between the local proxies of greater forces and ideologies preparing for greater conflict—our enemies with their Iranian trainers and Russian rockets, their veneration of martyrs and vision of a resurgent Islam; us with bourgeois aspirations and rifles stamped HARTFORD, CONN., USA. Suicide car bombs, roadside explosives, booby-trapped boulders, videotaped attacks, isolated outposts, hit-and-run, a modern military on hostile territory fighting a long, hopeless war against a weaker but more determined enemy for unclear and ultimately unattainable goals—before Iraq, before Afghanistan, there was this protracted affair in Lebanon. It is hardly possible to understand current events without understanding these ones, and yet they have been overlooked. Many thousands of Israeli men of Avi's generation, my generation, people whose awareness of the world blinked on around the interval between *Appetite for Destruction* and *Nevermind*, share the sense of owing an important part of our personalities to a time and place of no concern to anyone else, and to a war that never officially happened.

It will be clear to those familiar with the literature coming out of Israel in the past few thousand years that hilltops are considered places where the human and the divine might touch, and where great or terrible events might occur. There is Sinai, where God delivered his law to Moses. At Masada, a flat-topped hill in the desert along the Dead Sea, zealots who wouldn't surrender to Rome killed themselves before legionnaires breached the walls. There is Mount Moriah, where Abraham was said to have nearly sacrificed his heir Isaac in an incident whose legacy has ensured, according to one of the modern Hebrew poets, that their descendants are all "born with a knife in their heart." Tradition held that this hill was where God's spirit dwelled, so Solomon built a temple there, and Herod did too, before the Romans replaced it with a temple dedicated to Jupiter. The followers of Muhammad came to believe that this was the place where the Arabian prophet ascended to heaven in a mystic night journey, and thirteen hundred years ago they built an exquisite golden-domed shrine that stands today. There are a lot of stories about that hill, but this isn't one of them.

Traveling north, into Galilee, you pass Mount Gilboa, where Saul fell on his sword, and the hill north of the Sea of Galilee where a preacher addressed an audience in the early rumblings of a new religion and which adherents named the Mount of Beatitudes. To the west, along the coast, is Mount Carmel, where the prophet Elijah once challenged 450 priests of a rival god to a contest—each side would build an altar, and they would see whose deity could set it alight. This is where today the neighborhoods of Haifa spread above port cranes and industrial smokestacks. Moving farther north you cross a ridge that meets the sea in a warren of chalk grottoes, and then you're out of the modern state of Israel and in the mountainous south of Lebanon.

Inside Lebanon, three miles north of Israel's northernmost extremity, is a castle built by crusaders eight hundred years ago atop a sheer rock face. It's still known as Beaufort Castle, the name the crusaders chose. This story isn't about that hill either, but now we're close.

In the late 1960s border raids by Palestinian guerrillas from Lebanese territory started Israel's long Lebanon war in earnest—a war not with the state of Lebanon but with armed groups exploiting the weakness of the Lebanese government to their own ends. Over the years this conflict has changed in nature, and some of the participants have changed. It has more often been at the periphery of outside attention than at the center, but a wise observer keeps an eye on it always. It pauses on occasion but has never ended, and it is punctuated every so often by the tidal movements of our military back and forth across the frontier. It gained intensity in the mid- and late 1970s, when Avi and most of the other characters in this book were born, and has run parallel to our lives since then.

In June 1982 convoys of Israeli troops pushed into Lebanon, embarked on a misguided intervention with one of Lebanon's Christian factions. Soldiers captured Beaufort Castle from Palestinian fighters and turned it into a permanent military position. Israeli divisions rolled north toward Beirut and toward a morass that summer and fall that has been described by others. My interest here is in events that came later and have never been recorded, so I'll skip the earlier details: the attacks by Palestinian squads on civilian buses and schools inside Israel before the invasion; the army's devastating bombardment of Beirut in the summer of 1982 and the successful expulsion of the Palestine Liberation Organization; the way Israel decided this wasn't enough and attempted to force the installation of a friendly government in Lebanon, was foiled, saw its Christian allies massacre residents in two Palestinian refugee camps, and became embroiled in the Lebanese civil war. Israelis call this "sinking into the Lebanese mud."

In 1985, after protests at home and with dissent in the ranks, the army pulled back to the "security zone," a narrow strip of Lebanese land along the border. At this point the writing peters out, more or less, even though Israel remained there for fifteen more years.

After the invasion Israel found itself facing an enemy other than the one it thought it was fighting. These were not Palestinians but local Shiites calling themselves the Party of God, Hezbollah, funded and trained by the regime of the ayatollahs in Iran. These fighters appeared with new energies and a tactic, the suicide bomber, which turned out to be the signal innovation of the modern Middle East—the region's most notable contribution to our times, the perfect illustration of what it has done to itself. The men of Hezbollah grew in sophistication and strength, driven by the expertise, ideology, and cash of their Iranian patrons, feeding off the resentment caused by Israel's presence in Lebanon and riding the wave of religious war that had begun to crest in those years in this part of the world and which has now conclusively ravaged it. By the early 1990s the other armed groups had faded, Hezbollah had come into its own, the outline of the security zone war had been set, and the conditions had been created for our story.

The year 1994, when Avi was drafted, found the Israelis dug in at positions across the south of Lebanon: a perilous little world of hilltops peering at each other through binoculars and sending radio messages flitting back and forth over the canyons, like the bonfires relaying word of the new moon from Jerusalem over the summits in the rabbinic writings, "from the Mount of Olives to Sartaba, from Sartaba to Grofina, from Grofina to Hoveran, from Hoveran to Beit Baltin," and on to Babylon.

This was the security zone, from Mount Hermon in the east to the Mediterranean in the west. It was meant to keep guerrillas away from the border and protect the people of Israel's north: the frontier turkey farmers, the canners of corn and peas in urban factories, the Hebrew-speaking Arab plumbers, the beauties of Jewish Leningrad circa 1958, newly arrived in Israel with the great Soviet immigration and now lying on beaches near the Lebanon border, exposing their pale bodies to the unfamiliar ferocity of our sun.

The army gave the outposts pretty names like Basil, Crocus, Cypress, and Red Pepper. This reflects a floral preoccupation in our military, which in naming things generally avoids names like Hellfire or Apache in favor of ones like Artichoke, a night-vision apparatus for tank gunners, or Buttercup, an early-warning system for incoming mortar shells. In the jargon of army radiomen, wounded soldiers are "flowers." Dead soldiers are "oleanders." It isn't a code, because it isn't secret. Instead the names seem intended to bestow beauty on ugliness and to allow soldiers distance from the things they might have to describe. If you listened to the language of the Lebanon troops, you might have thought they occupied a kind of garden.

The Pumpkin was set up three miles due north of Beaufort Castle on a hilltop where nothing significant is known to have happened before the events recounted here or since. The military archives contain no record of the outpost's construction, or at least none I could find.

In Hebrew the outpost was called Dla'at—just Pumpkin, not *the* Pumpkin. But I have always thought of it as a place that deserves the definite article in English. As the Pumpkin's first historian in any language, and almost certainly its last, I grant myself license to call it in translation whatever I want. The name now seems to hint at the kind of magic at work in the transformation of a bare hilltop into the scene of emotion and drama and its sudden transformation back into a place of no importance at all.

# 8

AVI SAW THE green hills and valleys beyond the border and felt the first bite of the cold that came with altitude. The new arrivals thought about being in a foreign country, about what it meant to be surrounded by hostile territory. And then they were put to work.

Whatever heroic exploits existed in their imaginations, they discovered as all newcomers did that life at the Pumpkin was a matter of the grueling tasks necessary to maintain dozens of men on an isolated hill: washing pots, chopping vegetables, cleaning and greasing the machine guns, filling sandbags, an endless schedule of chores interrupted by turns in the guard posts and a few hours of sleep at night that were themselves interrupted by turns in the guard posts. Then Readiness with Dawn, and then it would all begin again.

What was the Pumpkin? A hilltop rectangle of earthen embankments the size of a basketball court. It was accessed by Israeli soldiers from the east on a road mined with some regularity and by the enemy from the west through several riverbeds that ran hidden from their towns up to the ridge.

The outpost was threatened by a guerrilla haunt in a nearby copse of terebinths and pines known as the Forest—a name that bore genuine menace in the soldiers' minds, although the vegetation was to a real forest as the placid puddle known as the "Sea" of Galilee is to a real sea or as the trickle of the "river" Jordan is to the Mississippi.

To the north the hilltops of the Ali Taher range continued through Outpost Red Pepper before terminating in a triangular peak capped with Outpost Cypress. Beaufort Castle was visible to the south, and in between was Outpost Citrus. These were the positions of the Red Line, the farthest extremity of the area under Israel's control.

Just to the west, outside the security zone and inside Lebanon proper, spread a plateau occupied by the Shiite town of Nabatieh. One day eleven years before, in 1983, an Israeli force had blundered through the town during the Shiites' most important religious festival, and the soldiers became surrounded by an angry crowd. They opened fire and killed two people, helping ensure the enmity of the Shiites and aiding the rise of their new military force, Hezbollah. Nabatieh was a guerrilla stronghold and the outpost's nemesis.

Peeking over a ridge to the south, past six miles of treacherous territory, representing home, were white houses in Metullah, the northernmost town in Israel.

The mood on the hill wasn't usually one of fear, though anyone might be forgiven for remembering it that way now. You can't be afraid all the time. The air at the Pumpkin was instead one of exhaustion and homesickness. It was not that the soldiers missed their cities or their friends, though of course that was part of it—they missed their real home, their parents' home, where everyone still lived. Army service here is the end of childhood, and going home meant that your father hugged you and your mother cooked you dinner, and the washing machine whirled green as you fell asleep in the room where you grew up.

At the outpost were several dozen young men isolated to a degree exceptional in the modern world. Mail arrived the same way the soldiers did, on convoys rendered unpredictable by the threat of bombs. There were no women. There was nothing feminine, nothing unnecessary to the purposes of allowing you to kill, preventing you from being killed, and keeping you from losing your mind in the meantime. Nothing was soft or smelled sweet.

Around the time of Avi's arrival in the fall of 1994 the outpost had one small bunker where soldiers were safe from shells and a few refurbished shipping containers in the yard, where they were not. Inside the containers were metal beds and filthy green mattresses.

There were a few Bedouin trackers, noncommissioned officers, who watched Hezbollah TV and Arabic movies in their little room between excursions to spot bombs along the road. A cook or two, with better-than-average food supplies that allowed the development of security zone delicacies like cornflakes doused in melted chocolate. A few infantry squads, two tank crews, a handful of field intelligence lookouts. The median age was no more than twenty, and the outpost commander was himself just a few years older.

Looking back on events we impose order, turning them into a story that makes sense to us. This is natural, and it's what I'm doing now. It becomes hard to remember what things felt like at the time, and not many people can. When Avi's platoon met recently, Ilya (he of *One Hundred Years of Solitude*) came up with an accurate description of what all of this was like when it was going on. It's worth

quoting here in full; unfortunately his deadpan, Slavic-inflected Hebrew must be left to the imagination.

"We were like sheep led to the slaughter," he said, and his friends
laughed. They seemed to have heard this from him before, probably
more than once.

> You do all kinds of nonsense, you don't know what you're
> doing—"Go there, go here, go there again tomorrow." I
> didn't know what I was doing. I washed dishes. [Laughter]
> They made me listen to all kinds of nonsense that they used
> to say there, all kinds of empty bullshit about this, about
> that, about whatever, and I didn't understand what they
> wanted from me. Sometimes we'd go to lay an ambush and
> lie there in the snow, the cold, I remember that. And that
> was it. That's what it was. It's all faded now. Now we're talk-
> ing about who shot what, he shot, the other guy shot, I don't
> remember who shot who. It was all chaos. I just remember
> these big green tables in the dining room that we had to
> scrub. [Laughter] That's all I remember.

# 9

It was the Pumpkin Incident, also known as the Flag Incident, that began the hill's brief period of notoriety and brought Avi up earlier than planned. He arrived with the uproar at its height.

One of the men there that day in October 1994 was a nineteen-year-old named Eran, who served with the engineering company of a different infantry brigade. This company's men alternated on the hill with the engineering company of the Fighting Pioneer Youth—four months inside, then four months of training in the desert, then back in.

Eran was doing his best to be a good soldier. He was of a type quite different than Avi. Today he speaks softly and tears up easily and without embarrassment. He doesn't dwell on these events. When he spoke about this, sitting on the roof of his apartment building in a Tel Aviv suburb, he said it was the first time he had mentioned the Pumpkin in many years. He has five children and works as a therapist. His specialty is trauma.

Readiness with Dawn ended without incident that morning. No one expected an incident. It had been years since guerrillas tried to storm an Israeli outpost, having realized that soldiers were more vulnerable outside their forts, on patrols or moving on the roads. The Pumpkin's fortifications were meager in those days, and the rules lax. You were still allowed to walk around outside without a helmet or flak jacket. No one had seen the guerrillas sneak up the ridge in the darkness. When a barrage began just after 8:30 a.m. no one panicked, because shelling was common. But this time it seemed worse than usual, and there was a new kind of percussion added to the crump of mortars—the rapid chatter of automatic rifles. This meant the enemy was close. The hill was under attack.

On the western side of the Pumpkin, the most dangerous side because it faced the hostile town, was the surveillance post, just a shipping container with a window that opened like a chow truck at a construction site. This was where two lookouts from a field intelligence unit sat with maps and binoculars, watching the houses and streets of the Lebanese. There was a smokescreen that could be triggered to protect them from missiles, at least that was the theory, but when someone activated it now the wind blew the smoke inside the outpost, blinding the defenders and making it hard to breathe. Neither Eran nor anyone else knew where the attackers were.

There were four soldiers on the western side—the two lookouts and two sentries from the infantry. But when the shooting became fierce the lookouts fled. One of them was seen running into the bunker below, and though he was physically unharmed he never recovered. That left the two infantrymen. One happened to be a medic, and when he heard there were casualties he decided to leave his post to treat them. The other sentry also vanished, and that's why there was no one guarding the approaches when the guerrillas arrived with their cameraman.

The world has become so used to this kind of thing that it's hard to imagine how potent it was when Hezbollah broadcast the jumpy footage of guerrillas with rifles and rocket launchers, shouting in Arabic, a sound track of martial music. Hezbollah understood that the images of an attack could be more important than the attack itself—this seems obvious now but wasn't at the time. It was the very beginning of videotaped violence and the media war, which is a war not for territory but for "consciousness."

In the video the Hezbollah cameraman starts out crouching in dry grass with a few of the fighters, his lens level with the spiky heads of dry milk thistles. The outpost is visible perhaps four hundred yards away, shell bursts blooming on the embankments. A voice off camera yells in Arabic, "Just a minute, just a minute," and then, as a smoke plume rises from the Pumpkin, someone shouts, "Good, good!" In the next shot the fighters are closer, taking cover behind a stone outcropping. You can see the Pumpkin a hundred yards away. Someone rises onto one knee and fires a rocket. The army used to find Hezbollah bodies in jeans and civilian jackets, but times had changed. These fighters are in uniform, with webbing and helmets. They appear capable.

Four guerrillas leave cover and begin to close the distance, running up the incline until they tire and begin to walk. The cameraman is behind them. When they have nearly reached the top they abruptly kneel. Someone has shouted a warning. There is an explosion to their left. They rise again, and one throws a grenade over the embankment and into the Pumpkin. Another raises a Hezbollah flag with both hands and plants it in triumph: it's Iwo Jima, or the moon landing.

That's where the video ends, so you don't see them turn around and run away.

The twenty-two-year-old lieutenant in charge of the Pumpkin got some of the soldiers organized and led them up to the trench that ran atop the embankments ringing the outpost. Another junior officer was moving in the trench when a shell fell behind him, and a soldier saw this officer sink to his knees, his expression that of a child in the moment between a scrape and the beginning of a wail. The officer's back was covered with blood, but when he realized he was alive and could move his limbs he composed himself. The soldier helped him down to the bunker, where they found medics treating someone who seemed to have lost his fingers.

By the time Eran made it up to the trench the flag was stuck in the embankment. The soldiers had mounted no effective response. Later they would be excoriated for their conduct in the press and in military tribunals, but in the confusion of the moment it's understandable that no one knew what to do.

The fire slackened and the worst seemed to be over. There was still shooting coming from the Forest, which was on the hilltop just to the south, and Eran raced through the trench until he faced the trees. Now that he could see the Forest, whoever was in the Forest could see him, and a few tracers zipped by his head. He crouched. Another soldier, a burly kid from one of the farming communities in the south of Israel, arrived at the same time and set himself up next to Eran just before a blast propelled Eran backward and filled the trench with smoke.

When he looked again the second soldier was on his back, a red pool spreading under his head. A third soldier ran up just then, and when he saw what had happened he fell to his knees and began hitting his head against the concrete wall of the trench. The dead soldier was his friend. Not long afterward the shelling stopped and the hill was quiet again.

According to an official Hezbollah account, the guerrillas captured the outpost, "purified it of Zionists," killed five soldiers, and "trampled the bodies beneath their feet," but this was nonsense. The outpost had lost a soldier, but it was still there, the garrison intact and functioning. The significance wasn't clear right away. That the TV images were the real weapons, that the Hezbollah fighters and Israeli soldiers had been turned into actors in an attack staged for the camera—these weren't things anyone understood yet.

The footage was broadcast across the Middle East and picked up by Israel's television stations. In the days that followed the Hezbollah man entered everyone's living room, raised his arms, and drove his flag in again and again. Israelis were horrified. Fear that we are no longer sufficiently tough is one of the key chemicals in our country's communal brain, and this explains the hysteria that followed the fixing of that little flag. The incident was taken to be not a small failure, the kind of thing that happens to garrisons whose senses are deadened by routine, but a sign of decay in the army and a frailty among Israel's youth. This became known as the Pumpkin Incident, the first time anyone in Israel had heard the outpost's name.

Another important thing to know about this country is that we tend to see either unadulterated victory or disaster. So this was a disaster. It assumed the dimensions of a major military defeat, and headline writers began calling it "the Disgrace." The army kicked a few soldiers out of Eran's unit and declared the young officer in charge unfit for command.

Israeli society and its military were changing, the collective receding and the individual coming to the fore, and the flag became a focus for people's unease. Some thought part of the blame lay with the growing involvement of parents in their children's army service: it was becoming common in those days for mothers to call their sons' commanders to lodge complaints, a collision between one of the country's most important institutions, the army, and its most important institution, the family. Or perhaps, some suggested, it had to do with tolerance for soldiers crying at military funerals—there was a debate in those days about whether this was appropriate. "When fear and crying become respectable subjects that are discussed and encouraged, it's hard to get angry at soldiers in an isolated post," wrote one journalist.

Back in Israel, two of Eran's comrades were hitchhiking at an intersection when a man pulled up, identified their uniform insignia, and said, "You're the cowards, right?" One of the soldiers leaned into the car window and punched him in the face.

# 10

IN THE SAME week of the Pumpkin Incident the newspapers were reporting a triumphant visit by our prime minister to the king of Morocco in Casablanca. A front-page article was headlined "A Bank, Not a Tank." Reading the headlines from those days in late October and November 1994 is like reading the journal entries of a child you can barely recognize as yourself or one of those notebooks people keep beside their bed to record their dreams. The word *peace* was used without irony. Peace! Now it feels like the word *telegraph* or *wedlock*—a curio. This was, as I've mentioned, the heyday of the euphoria over the new Middle East.

Some decided that the Pumpkin Incident was linked to the anticipated arrival of peace. "The fighting spirit has been broken," wrote one analyst of the soldiers who had abandoned their posts on the hill, "because no one wants to be a war's last fatality, and many feel that the 100 Years' War is about to be over." Should we laugh at this line, or weep?

A new Middle East was being born just then, but not the one anyone imagined. It was happening in the scrub among boulders and concrete fortifications on a hill in the south of Lebanon. Only a few young people were present for the delivery.

# 11

A FEW WEEKS after the Pumpkin Incident and not long after Avi arrived on the hill, guerrillas ambushed an army convoy coming from Israel. They emerged from the houses of a village that cowered beneath Beaufort Castle, and then they disappeared back inside. This village, Arnoun, was directly on the line between the security zone and Lebanon proper, caught on a border not of its making and battered and half deserted as a result.

Avi's company commander was Yohai, one of those rare officers with an instinctive understanding of young soldiers and a clear idea of what to do always, the idea generally being to attack. Yohai had identified Avi as a soldier who did not automatically obey orders; the commander appreciated this quality. When news of the convoy came Yohai didn't wait for orders. He just rounded up Avi and a few others, took two armored vehicles, swung onto the dirt road that led south along the ridge, and headed for the fighting.

When they reached the village they went room by room through two abandoned houses near where the guerrillas had been seen. The soldiers went in shooting and throwing grenades. No one was there. Outside, Avi raised his rifle and fired his pretty grenades with their champagne-cork pop, followed a moment later by the thud of the explosion, narrowly missing an Israeli officer of high rank who had appeared from somewhere to join the action.

When the soldiers burst into the next house through a fresh shell hole in the wall it was clear that people lived there. There were couches, carpets, a fridge. You never trained on houses that looked like that and it felt strange, but there was nothing to do be done, so Avi and the others swept the rooms upstairs, throwing grenades and following their barrels through the doors as they had been taught.

Yohai headed down a staircase toward a small room that opened to his left, and inside he found a young man crouching in the corner, looking up at him and holding a grenade launcher, and Yohai squeezed his trigger but the gun jammed, and they just looked at each other. Yohai's number two was coming through the doorway after him, pushing him in, and Yohai had to shove him back out—the whole thing lasted a second, but it seemed much longer. When they got out Yohai threw grenades through the door and then had a tank fire a few shells through the wall, and when they went back in they found two dead guerrillas. The second was in another corner, and Yohai hadn't noticed.

Avi was sent to the vehicles for a stretcher, and as he sprinted off he made a discovery. He always thought that when engaged in combat you wouldn't get tired, that supernatural forces would kick in and the regular rules wouldn't apply. But it was downhill to the vehicles and uphill coming back, and he slowed and was winded and walking by the time he returned. This was the kind of detail he noticed.

# 12

AVI WASN'T SURE he could handle this sort of thing, no one is until it happens, but it turned out he was fine. He told Yossi so the next time he made it home. Yossi was Avi's father. He had once been in the Fighting Pioneer Youth himself and had helped capture the Old City of Jerusalem from the Jordanians in 1967. He withstood Egyptian bombardments in the Suez Canal outposts after that war—the worst were the 60 mm shells, he remembers, which were inaudible until just before they hit. Then he fought across the canal after the reversals of 1973. There is nothing military about Yossi. He's a smiling man despite everything, compact like Avi. One day he was back from Suez in his kitchen with Avi's mother, Raya, and older brother, an infant at the time. The baby's bottle thumped to the floor, and the young family contemplated Yossi flat on his stomach with his hands covering his head.

Yossi knew about such matters and was worried about his son. Avi said he didn't mind the shelling. What he did mind was going out in front on patrol with the metal probe that engineers use to poke the ground and spot mines and booby traps. Yossi wasn't sure if this was for the obvious reason or because when they had been taught to use the probe in engineers' training Avi might have been elsewhere with a cigarette and a novel.

Avi arrived at an agreement with Raya. If something happened on the hill, he would use the single phone line at the outpost to call home. He would say only, "Everything's okay." That would mean that everything was not okay but Avi was, and the family would know he was alive by the time anything was reported on the radio a few hours later. In those years the radio announcers in Israel would report "heavy exchanges of fire" in Lebanon, and that was a code—it meant soldiers were dead but this couldn't be reported yet because their families hadn't been informed. Everyone understood, and if you had a son in Lebanon you had a few difficult hours before things became clear, after which either things went back to normal or life as you knew it ended.

Avi smoked cigarettes and toasted sandwiches on the little spiral heaters with bread and processed cheese pilfered from the kitchen. There were occasional interruptions of the drudgery. The platoon was supposed to set off on an ambush one frigid evening, for example, lying in wait for guerrillas in bushes near the outpost from nightfall to dawn; these excursions were one of the garrison's regular missions. But the infantry gods decided the platoon had suffered enough and sent white flakes to bury the hill. The operation was canceled. For kids from the Middle East snow is a novelty, and there is a photograph showing Avi and the others grinning in the flurry, their surroundings forgotten.

But mostly it was cleaning dishes and guns, waiting out shelling and standing on guard duty, crawling into his sleeping bag with his boots on and closing his eyes—and then it was Readiness with

Dawn and he was on his feet again. They were more exhausted than they had ever been. They wanted to go home. They were tired of everything. Their *dicks were broken*, to use one of the crucial terms in the parlance of our military—one which, despite its importance in describing a key stage and mood in our lives, does not appear in the great dictionary of modern Hebrew compiled by Eliezer Ben-Yehuda and does not originate, as much of our language does, in any of the books of the Bible.

Occasionally their platoon leader would round them up and deliver inane speeches to them in the rain, or so they remembered, perhaps unkindly. He wasn't much older than they were, and was no match for them. They called him the Peacock and tried to make his life as difficult as possible. Avi thought bitterly of himself and his friends as "hewers of wood and drawers of water"—Joshua 9:27.

# 13

Morning will rise soon here in Lebanon, and fog will cover the land again. Only the hilltops will be visible above it, a view that is cold and enchanted like the set of a play, or a picture from a story or a fantasy film.

Avi was sitting in the outpost before dawn, writing a letter. Nearly a year had gone by since he first arrived on the hill. He was back for another tour. In this description of the beginning of a day at the Pumpkin it is possible to see his powers of observation beginning to sharpen, the flexing of literary muscles.

To the south, playing the role of the bad guy, is Beaufort Castle, haughty, dark and threatening above the mist. Afterward the sun will start to come up and paint the sky beyond Mount Hermon many shades of pink and red, turning the fog into a white and unthreatening carpet. In the end the sun will finally rise entirely and reveal itself, the fog will dissipate, and once again we will see Lebanon, beautiful and wild.

The nighttime sounds of the Pumpkin: the hiss of a radio, a few words passing through the ether from another hilltop, footsteps as a dark figure passes in battle dress.

Again and again I find myself amazed by the power of the landscape in this place, by the contrast between the hills, the valleys and wadis, a contrast so great it is almost impossible to calculate. The villages and towns here are also a puzzling mosaic sometimes. On one hill you see a village with a big church and a red tower, which makes the village look European, and opposite are typical Arab houses. New villas opposite churches, and old houses (from the previous century, some of them, or at least from the beginning of this one) next to new high-rises.

Letters from the Pumpkin went down to Israel on the armored convoys and then through an army office into the regular mail and thus to the homes of the girls to whom the soldiers unburdened themselves and from whom they hoped to receive—to receive what? Understanding, certainly. Respect. Just the right dosage of pity. And, when they got home, who knows? These letters were the most important personal records produced at the outpost, but most of them are lost now. Few of these relationships lasted, and who can blame the girls, forced to wait for unpredictable, intense letters and an unpredictable, intense person who showed up briefly full of incomprehensible experiences he wanted to talk about and not talk about, and then disappeared again. You can't just call her up today, now that both of you are other people, and ask for your letters back.

Avi's writing was in the form of letters to a girl he had known since the first grade. Her name was Smadar. She remembered him as a child constantly in trouble, exiled from classrooms into hallways, asking questions of teachers that occasionally won him esteem exceeding their exasperation.

Even when she and Avi had grown up he took nothing for granted. Their friends would always meet at the same place when they returned from the army on weekends, and he wanted to know why. Why not somewhere else? When they were about to go out one evening Avi saw Smadar putting on makeup and asked her why. It was dark outside, and did she think anyone would notice?

Everything here is a kind of illusion. Opposite the place where I am sitting, on a hill, is a beautiful villa with a large garden and red shingles. It's a pastoral scene. But if you look closely, you see the bullet holes all over the house, and you see that the garden is neglected because no one dares live there, in such dangerous proximity to the outpost.

It's very hard for me to put my finger precisely on the feeling I have when I'm here. It's a kind of sadness mixed with longing so deep that sometimes it's painful. And fear, of course. It's strange, but the fear doesn't bother me at all. It's part of the sadness and the longing. It's with me all the time, but not directly, kind of sneaking up on me. That's how it appears when you're alone. I mean not when you're literally alone, but when I step away for a second and think about home, about my friends, or about a love story I haven't started yet.

This was around the time that a copy of *Reality Bites* reached the outpost, when for a while one of the voices heard in the bunker belonged to Winona Ryder. It was also not long after the company commander—Yohai, the fighter who stormed the house with Avi the year before—was on his way up to the trench during a barrage when shrapnel sheared off his nose and cut an artery in his neck. He got himself to one of the bunkers. There was a soldier at the doorway who just stared at him and froze, because Yohai was like their father, he was supposed to be taking care of them, but here he was scorched and stunned with his nose hanging by a piece of skin. Yohai walked past the soldier into the bunker and lay on one of the beds. He called for a medic and blacked out. The medics say he was flailing around so much they had to drug him just to get a tube in his mouth and keep him breathing until a helicopter could land. They did a good job, so he's alive today. He sends his regards.

# 14

Until this time, no one from Avi's company had yet been killed or badly wounded. The bad luck, the soldiers believed, belonged to the second unit that alternated on the hill, the one where Eran served, the one humiliated by the flag. This second unit, returned to the line in the spring of 1995, lost a rifleman and two trackers in an ambush among nearby olive trees. The Fighting Pioneer Youth, on the other hand, started to think they were protected, at least until their commander was hit—that was when the truth began to dawn on them, though of course no one knew the extent of it.

Before returning to Avi it would be useful to devote a few more words to Eran, whom we left in the trench after the flag incident, watching a soldier lying very still. The way Eran's time at the Pumpkin ended is worth describing.

Five months after the Pumpkin Incident, the rotation of the two units sent Avi's company down to Israel for training and brought Eran back to the hill. At around this time Eran was trying to arrive at a view of the world that would help him make sense of everything and allow him to function in light of what he had seen. He had come to the crisis John Prine sings about in "Angel from Montgomery":

"Just give me one thing that I can hold on to / To believe in this living is just a hard way to go."

What Eran had in his brain up to that point—loyalty to his friends, the moderate religion of his parents, a few vague ideas about his country—was not enough. He needed an idea. This led him to a store in Tel Aviv where they sold the writings of a rabbi, Yehuda Leib Ashlag, whose readings of Kabbalah and Marx led him in the 1930s to a kind of mystic socialism. Eran picked up a pamphlet called *The Book of the Giving of the Torah*, in which the rabbi argued that altruism was at the center of the Jewish religion. "We must understand that all of the commandments of the Torah are no more and no less than the sum of the details to be found in the one commandment 'Love thy neighbor as thyself,'" wrote the rabbi, echoing a much older lesson taught by the sages.

Altruism, like everything else, proceeded in steps, he wrote: first you love your immediate family and then your more distant relatives; then you learn to love your country and then the whole world. True altruism becomes possible in the third stage, because when you are part of a nation you give to people you don't know. That is why the Torah was given not to Abraham, Isaac, or Jacob, who were just patriarchs of an extended family, but much later, to Moses in the desert of Sinai, when the Hebrews had become a nation of hundreds of thousands.

The rabbi agreed with much of Marx's thinking, though he observed that the implementation of this thinking in Soviet Russia showed that people weren't ready yet. But he was optimistic. Humanity, he wrote, is "climbing up as if on the steps of a ladder," and this was the thinking behind Marxism and also behind the Torah;

*The Ladder* was the name of the rabbi's most important book. He identified two forces at work in the machine of human development. One, egotism, is a negative force that leads people to take care of themselves and destroy their neighbor, and the other, altruism, is a positive force whose highest expression is giving to others without expectation of receiving anything in return. "The egoistic force acts like the centripetal force, pulling things from outside a person and concentrating them inside himself," he wrote in one of his essays, "and the altruistic force is like centrifugal forces, flowing from the inside of his body outside; these two forces are to be found in every part of creation according to its substance, and also in the human being according to his substance."

Eran brought the pamphlet to the outpost, kept it in his webbing, and read it when he could, sitting on the soiled mattresses under fluorescent lights, sneaking a cigarette in the yard between tasks, flicking the ash between his scuffed boots. He divided the men at the Pumpkin into two groups: the ones trying to do the minimum and make it home safe, and the idealists, who were committed to something larger than themselves. In hours spent arguing with the others about this he forged the following conclusion: He was there not for himself, not for the respect he received when he returned home, and not even for his friends. He was there *for the country*. This was the highest altruism he could imagine from where he stood. He volunteered for everything.

Before first light one day, someone shook Eran awake and told him to take over one of the guard posts for Readiness with Dawn. Eran didn't think it was his turn, and he was exhausted, so he argued and tried to go back to sleep. In the end he was forced to concede.

He loaded his rifle and trudged up the stairs to the dark trench, angry with himself for resisting. He was here for the country, and his own fatigue should have no meaning. He had been weak, and in his memory this is how he left the Pumpkin—after descending a step on the ladder, after letting himself down. The night sky lightened.

A few hours before, around 3 a.m., a lookout using a thermal camera at the Pumpkin's surveillance post had seen seven figures leave Nabatieh, the Shiite town, on foot. The lookout was certain they were guerrillas. They were heading for the lower end of one of the riverbeds that led up toward the Pumpkin. Once they were in the riverbed they would be hidden from view, so he decided to ask permission from headquarters in Israel to open fire quickly with one of the outpost's tanks. Permission was necessary in such cases because the guerrillas were still outside the security zone and the army was worried about killing civilians by mistake, which was not uncommon. The lookout got on the radio:

*Hoshen, this is Ataf 4.*

("Ataf 4" was the lookout, whose name was Amir. "Hoshen" was the soldier at headquarters in Israel, a young woman Amir's age; as it happened, the two knew each other from civilian life, and she never forgot the conversation. "Dirties" are guerrillas.)

*Ataf 4, this is Hoshen, over.*

*Receive: A confirmed ID of seven dirties in the southern outskirts of Nabatieh.*

*Roger. Do you have the coordinates?*

*I'm giving it to you on the [telephone]. . . . Requesting permission to open fire.*

*Roger, hold on. . . . Ataf 4, this is Hoshen.*

*This is Ataf 4. Do we have permission to fire?*

*Negative.*

*What do you mean, negative? We have a certain ID of seven dirties. They're going into the riverbed. Soon we're not going to be able to hit them. I request permission to fire now.*

*This is Hoshen. Negative. No permission to fire.*

*Hoshen, this is Ataf 4. Then what the hell am I doing here?*

The guerrillas disappeared.

When shells began falling at 5:59 a.m. Eran thought he saw a few heads peeking from behind boulders downhill. He fired at them and saw puffs of dust nearby. Then he was on his knees. He couldn't breathe. Something had flashed and something was burning. He looked down and saw that his right arm was no longer attached to his body but remained in the sleeve of his coat. He dragged himself out of the guard post and into the trench, where he found himself looking at someone's boots. Help me, Eran said.

Two soldiers found him charred and delirious. They put a tourniquet on the stump and carried him down to one of the bunkers, which by some magic appeared to have assumed the size of an auditorium, so he remembers. They laid him on the floor between the beds. A medic named Davidoff gave him a shot in the thigh—morphine. Eran felt he had to scream, he just needed to get it out of him, so he screamed and screamed, and then he said, I'm sorry.

The garrison radioed down to Israel that they had flowers and needed a thistle quickly to evacuate them, but the shelling made it too risky for helicopters, so the soldiers loaded Eran onto an armored vehicle and drove him down the hill and out of mortar range. When he was finally placed on a helicopter someone arranged his severed arm atop his chest. Next to him was the lookout, Amir, who had been running along the trench and must have passed behind Eran's emplacement just as the rocket hit. The lookout was now a motionless human shape under a gray blanket. He was twenty years old. A few months earlier, before heading to the Pumpkin for the first time, Amir had written in a neat hand on a yellow pad, "In a few days I'll be on my way to another outpost. It is a road that might be one-way, or might not be." His mother found the note afterward.

When the helicopter landed in Israel men in white smocks rushed Eran through sliding doors into an emergency room, and a TV cameraman filmed him going past. In the footage you see the altruist's face blackened and unrecognizable, and hear him screaming something as he passes. If you pay attention you can make out the words: "For the country."

# 15

AVI WROTE A letter to Smadar one night from the war room, a tiny space with a few chairs, radios, and blue cups sticky with the residue of tea. The army had recently completed one of its periodic offensives in Lebanon, a few weeks of shelling and air strikes and belligerent rhetoric after which everything remained as it had been before. Avi was at home when the offensive began and was in no hurry to get back. But his father, who didn't want him to incur the wrath of his superiors, pushed him to go and finally drove him north to catch a convoy. This ride inspired Avi to write a story, later lost, comparing it to Isaac's walk with Abraham up Mount Moriah.

Smadar had a boyfriend at the time who was not Avi. But they read the same books, and her intellect matched his. His letters to her, he once wrote, were a way to "calm my internal combustion." She loved his writing, and he knew it. Even then, Smadar had a look that suggested she could fathom all kinds of things and that these things might include you. She thought Avi seemed much older than he was because he read so much and had lived two lives in parallel—his own and that of an observer watching himself.

Avi was thinking about a change in his life. His life was not his to change, stuck as he was on a hilltop in an enemy country. But Avi did not accept this, or accepted it only as a transient injustice. He thought he might move his things out of his parents' house in one of the Haifa suburbs and live somewhere else by himself.

The young Avi was a great analyst of his own thoughts and actions. This was one of the things that made being intimate with him so tiring, and it is also one of the common characteristics of a writer. He was aware of making an effort to maintain a barbed exterior while hanging on to something of his childhood, hoarding a small supply of innocence in the hope that it would survive until his discharge, upon which he would recover it. This was an idea from *The Kites*, the part where Romain Gary tells us that the kite maker Ambroise Fleury, a veteran of the Great War, was wise enough in his youth to hide a particle of innocence that he protected through the horrors of the trenches and which had evolved over the years into a kind of wisdom. Ambroise's kites, for Gary, were beautiful flights of the imagination, acts of creativity representing the best of what humans can produce; one of the airborne contraptions is in the shape of Jean-Jacques Rousseau, "with wings made to look like two books, the wind ruffling their pages."

"Now I am keeping it in hiding, so no one here finds it," wrote Avi of his own store of innocence. "If they find it they won't hesitate to use it against me, and it will be hard to make it through the time I have remaining in uniform. There is no room for innocence here. Innocence brings exploitation in this place."

Avi knew he had an acute sensitivity to other people and knew this was not entirely a blessing. He found it hard to accept the imperfections he saw in others and in himself. For him the army was, more than anything else, an intensive course on human nature, and it was changing him. "I can't see people the same way I did at first— wonderful or terrible, little or big. Now they're a jumble of good and evil, small-mindedness and greatness," he wrote. "The point is that we are changing (and this is what scares me most) into mediocre people, people who meet halfway, and it affects us all in nearly every aspect of life," he wrote. "It affects our little choices and our big ones. Today you won't see the world as you did before. You won't make the clearer distinctions. You'll compromise." The version of himself that once stood with the others in the yard at the training base was an innocent child with big dreams. Now he felt he was not a child and not innocent. "My dreams today are much smaller and simpler," he wrote, "and I might even realize them." He was starting to think about the book he would write.

Can we imagine Gary as a companion for the young and lonely Avi of those days, drawn by the presence of his books in the soldier's rucksack, flying nocturnal circles over the Pumpkin in an invisible biplane? Here is Gary on those members of the French military who, unlike him, surrendered and collaborated in 1940: "I understood, only too well, those who refused to follow de Gaulle," he wrote in a memoir that Avi hadn't read. "They had learned wisdom, that poisoned draught with its sickly taste of humility, renunciation and acceptance, which the habit of living drips, drop by drop, down our throats." The habit of living—that is, adulthood—this is what Avi was figuring out during those nights at the edge of the world.

# 16

ONE DAY IN the early summer of 1996 a reporter arrived at the Pumpkin with a few senior officers. "Not many journalists come here," the reporter wrote, "especially not this year. The outpost's soldiers hold one of the most dangerous parts of the 'red line,' the random, winding, gap-ridden border of the security zone.

> I am reminded of the Suez Canal outposts in the early '70s. Then, as now, the fighters are brave, the construction is of reinforced concrete, and the military and political concept is a matter of debate. . . .
>
> Go speak to the soldiers, an officer of high rank encourages me, as we stand under a concrete roof in the center of the outpost. They're tough—combat soldiers. But with a bit of prodding they open up and will pour their hearts out.
>
> Pour their hearts out? The soldiers laugh. They are thin—skin, bone and muscle. What are you waiting for, they say. Insert your ammunition clip, the one with all of the usual questions reporters ask. We know them by heart. We already have the answers. You probably want to hear, "We're afraid

but doing the job as best we can," or "We're here so Galilee can sleep quietly," and that we "miss home but want to make Hezbollah hurt." There, we said it. Take a picture, write something down, and go home, Dad.

That summer it seemed that Avi's soul had not only left the Pumpkin but had departed the Middle East entirely. He was thinking about his travels after his discharge the following spring. He was interested in India and the Far East, which was where most Israeli kids headed after the army was done with them. But the destination he really had in mind was Europe: first to Scandinavia, where he thought he would feel like a dwarf surrounded by giants and where the politeness of the locals would do him good, and after that to Ireland, a green country full of legends and fanatic Christianity, "a country of contradictions, just like me." He liked how Ireland was placed a little to the side, "next to Britain but not contaminated with her ills." He had never been to Ireland; except for time spent abroad with his family when he was in kindergarten, Avi had never left Israel. But he could picture it clearly. Smadar, to whom he confided this plan, could already envision him in a pub in that country, puffing a pipe over the manuscript of a novel full of cynical humor and philosophy.

And from there to the most distant place he could imagine: Alaska. You could see him there too, a glass of whisky on a rough desk, somewhere in the interior accessible by snowmobile or Piper, surrounded by that precious resource our country lacks, emptiness. He would take the concrete and officers and guerrillas who once jailed him on a hilltop in a land far away, citizens of a conflict impossible for him to imagine now, the people who tried every day to find and destroy that last reserve of his innocence, and he would turn them all into a story.

Avi put this plan into a letter once. But when he was still on the Alaska part Bono came on the radio: "Is it getting better, or do you feel the same?" Avi was under the spell of that song as much as anyone. He put down his pen, lit a cigarette, and allowed his thoughts to drift.

# 17

IN THOSE DAYS the Lebanese underbrush was full of Israelis, soldiers waiting for guerrillas on hillsides and in riverbeds. This was
the ambush, the army's main offensive tactic in the security zone.
Sometimes the soldiers stayed for days or even a week, camouflag-
ing themselves in bushes, taking turns sleeping, eating chocolate and
shitting in plastic bags spread over upside-down helmets and pissing
in bottles that they had to carry out with them afterward. Sometimes
there were guerrillas waiting in the same bushes, and they killed the
soldiers. Sometimes the soldiers killed one another. In one incident
a platoon leader moving at night at the front of a line doubled back,
the men at the rear thought he was a guerrilla and opened fire, the
platoon leader thought they were guerrillas and returned fire, and
one soldier was dead and a few wounded by the time they figured
out what happened.

In the middle of June a squad of thirteen at the Pumpkin began
preparing for an ambush in the Forest, where they were to spend the
night overlooking one of the riverbeds leading up from the Shiite
town. The riverbed, invisible to the Israeli lookouts, was used by the

guerrillas to move up the ridge, where they could attack the outpost or mine the convoy road.

Avi wasn't among the soldiers to depart with the ambush team that night. He was assigned to man the radios in the war room, so he experienced what ensued through the shouting on the frequencies, the gunfire audible from a few hundred yards away, the panic as rescue teams sprinted out, and of course the disbelief the next morning when only one of the original thirteen walked back in. It was then that the Fighting Pioneer Youth's engineering company truly understood their luck had changed. A slight soldier named Yaacov, who now lives in a Toronto suburb, was there and remembers it in sharp detail, and there are also a few scraps in the military archives. Avi was a veteran by this time, but Yaacov was inexperienced. It was his first tour.

Yaacov was given a new nightscope that could be attached to his helmet and swiveled onto one eye. When he turned it on he saw the other soldiers in green. He was also given a pack of medical equipment that felt like a refrigerator on his back. They followed the dirt road that left the Pumpkin heading south, skirting the Forest at first. After a few hundred yards they came to a curve in the road that was known as the Falcon Bend. This is why the night's events were referred to afterward as the Falcon Incident.

They left the road at the Falcon Bend and headed west into the underbrush, picking their way up toward the ridgeline. There was a small Israeli minefield here left over from years ago, a safe route through it marked with white stones.

The officer went ahead to check the ambush spot, then motioned the others into position. It was a cold night, and Yaacov put on a jacket and stuffed a heat bag between his legs. They sat quietly, leaning back on their helmets. Every so often the sergeant kicked Yaacov hard, thinking he was asleep. He wasn't, but he was so new he wasn't allowed to complain. Wisps of fog blew in, and it became harder to see. He considered the stones by his feet, the dark vegetation around them. At 4:30 a.m. the officer signaled that it was time to return to the outpost.

Yaacov rolled onto his side and emptied his bladder, but the ground was uneven and his heavy pack nearly flipped him over. He only narrowly avoided a hygienic accident. By the time he buttoned up, the front of the squad was moving. Yaacov, at the back of the line with the sergeant, felt relief at the renewed movement of his limbs. Three guerrillas who had been waiting for them in one of the bushes raised their rifles.

The officer at the front saw something and shouted an order, but Yaacov never knew what he said. Yaacov dropped, the pack bringing him down hard. His kneecap cracked. He heard automatic thumping and explosions and yelling, and also groaning coming from the ground nearby. He threw off his pack and got up, heard bullets hit around him, and sprinted toward an outcropping where some of the others were shooting from cover to help him make it. Red tracers flew by his head and just as he arrived something hit him like a hammer moving at the speed of sound. There was smoke coming from a hole in the sleeve of his coat. His fingers were weak and the butt of his rifle had disappeared.

A machine gun lay on the ground nearby. Next to it was its owner, who called out to Yaacov: Put a tourniquet on me, my hand's gone. But bullets were still hissing through the vegetation and pinging off the rocks, and Yaacov was too scared to move, so he pulled a rubber tourniquet from his pocket and threw it at the wounded man. An explosion illuminated the scene for a moment. By now Yaacov's nightscope was useless because there was too much light in the eastern sky, which was going from black to gray as if nothing were out of the ordinary.

Tourniquet, the gunner was crying, and Yaacov saw he had no choice. He put down a grenade he had been gripping in his fist and crawled over. The soldier's forearm was pumping blood onto the ground. Yaacov had never seen anything like it. He managed to get the tourniquet on, and then he saw a figure running from the battle heading west toward the Shiite town. The figure was only a few dozen yards away when Yaacov aimed. But then he hesitated. He had been taught that soldiers wore helmets and guerrillas did not, so anyone without a helmet was a guerrilla and you were supposed to shoot. The figure had no helmet. But what if, Yaacov thought, one of the soldiers lost his helmet, became confused, and started running in the wrong direction? He couldn't pull the trigger, and the sergeant next to him fired instead. The running man dropped. He turned out to be the guerrillas' machine gunner. He had charged the Israelis, shooting until his gun jammed or his ammunition was gone, and then threw his weapon aside and tried to make it home. His name was Bilal. He died, but I would encounter his smiling face later on. Back at the Pumpkin mortars were falling, and Avi had left the war room to organize men around the perimeter in case the skirmish was a diversion for an attack on the base itself.

Yaacov headed back in the direction the squad had come the

evening before, walking backward and shooting at bushes. He stepped on something soft and jumped—it was one of the radiomen, who had been a cook and then volunteered for combat. His mouth was open and emitting red foam. A rescue team seemed to have arrived from the outpost, and one of the new soldiers was staring at someone else lying on the ground. Of course everyone knew each other very well, maybe better than they had ever known anyone outside their family. Yaacov crouched next to the prone figure, lifted an arm, and felt for a pulse. He's dead, Yaacov said. Help someone else.

Shut up, shut up, said the staring soldier, and Yaacov moved on. He found another soldier carrying someone who had had not a drop of blood visible on him but who was also dead; the soldier walked a few more paces and put him down. The officer was nearby. He was dead too. Yaacov got close to the road and passed the squad's second radioman writhing on the ground, his webbing emitting smoke. The sergeant had also been hit, and someone was dressing his shoulder.

Soldiers coming from the Pumpkin were rushing into the underbrush with stretchers, including one of Avi's friends, a medic, who remembers kneeling and pressing his fingers under jawbones looking for a pulse—nothing, nothing, nothing—and his medical supplies running out, and then jeeps arriving with more medics. But he doesn't remember any sound. In his memory this all happened in perfect silence.

Besides Yaacov, only one other soldier was still walking. It became clear that this soldier's mind had been scratched, as they say in the army, and he thought his friends were trying to kill him. He was helped into a jeep, and now only Yaacov was left. He was aware of the ache in his arm, but it wasn't too bad. It was light enough now for him to see that the rest of the squad was scattered horizontal at the Falcon Bend.

At the outpost Avi heard news of flowers and oleanders come over the radio. The faces of the men at the Pumpkin were drained of color. He got a turn on the phone and dialed, and his father answered. "Everything's okay," Avi said.

# 18

I have the feeling that everything is disintegrating, everything is falling, everything I know is changing inexorably and all of the principles of life are collapsing. I need to find some kind of definition for how to proceed, otherwise I don't think I'll be able to find any kind of way forward at all.

That is Avi writing to Smadar the next day. His thoughts are in disarray, and his descriptive touch has deserted him. He needs her to listen but can't bring himself to write something he wants to say to her. He seems young. This was just after the men from the ambush squad were sent south to Israel—eight for treatment, including Yaacov, and five for burial.

He knew them all, of course, though none were from his own platoon. Some of his friends tried to convince themselves that though the unit was clearly no longer favored by God or luck, the platoon still was. You had to believe something. Avi didn't believe it. "His discovery of danger does not come at once; often it does not come for a long time," wrote one Great War veteran of a soldier's experience of fear. "At first he has a strange feeling of invulnerability—a form of egotism—then it is suddenly brought home to him that he is not a spectator but a bit of the target, that if there are casualties he may be one of them." This was now apparent. Having other plans would not be enough to save him.

The guard posts were manned, the guns oiled, the pots washed. The life of that hill never paused. The outpost commander believed routine was the only thing that would save his men, and was planning to send a new squad to the very same spot that night to make a point. The men cursed him for it, though some of them appreciated him more later in their lives. In the background was Pink Floyd.

Do you remember when we talked about your way? It was kind of, "Let It Be," so I tried. I really tried, but now I can't continue trying to think like that, it just doesn't fit. I'm almost 21 and I've seen so much violence, so much blind cruelty, dreams shattered, lives cut short suddenly and without warning or sign. . . .

Now the tape deck is playing "Wish You Were Here," and how I wish you were here! One thing is hard for me and probably always will be—putting into action what I want. I never succeed in expressing that level of my personality, the same level, by the way, that is located near a few other things that I can't manage to reveal, and that's a shame. It's like a crystal—every time you move it you see a different beam of light, and it's almost impossible to find the precise spot from which you can see your beam.

That's it for now. My fuel has simply run out.

I already miss everything.

Avi

This was the Falcon Incident of June 1996, one of those "short, bloody, spasmodic silent fights which could be followed on no maps and are recorded nowhere, except in some mother's heart." That description is from Romain Gary, who was talking about different battles, but it is apt.

# 19

THAT FALL AVI mentally discharged himself, though his body still had a few months to go in uniform and continued to report for duty. Time at the end of your service slows down. It becomes torture to wake up, sometimes after dreaming that you're free, and to see green—that dreadful color—and to remember that you aren't after all.

Avi decided to spend his brief leaves in Tel Aviv and answered an ad looking for a third roommate to rent an apartment in the city. The others were girls from the university. It was unusual for someone still in uniform to move out of his parents' home. In the accepted order of things this is a stage reached only later, but Avi couldn't wait. ("When I get out I intend to devour life," he wrote to Smadar after the Falcon Incident, "to do and try everything, to live fast and know as much as I can. Because you can't know when it will end.") The three roommates hung pictures together and fixed a few health hazards, and then they moved in with hand-me-down chairs, pans, and posters.

Avi still spent most of his time in the army. But when he was given furloughs that winter he split the time between his parents' home, where he took part in the raucous and argumentative Sabbath dinners that he didn't like to miss, and the apartment in the city, where he celebrated his unilateral emancipation. He had philosophical discussions with his roommates over dinner. They sat playing guitar and singing the hits of the early nineties, the ones they remembered from high school. They went to the Tel Aviv clubs; the scene wasn't what it is now, but it was warming up. They made *jahnoun*. Avi's two older brothers were university students, and they stopped by. He was happy.

What happens is that you're a high-school student and the child of your parents, and then you're a member of a unit in the army, and these aren't identities you choose, and then you get out and start trying new ones. You travel and test a few different versions of yourself, maybe a bit wilder or more considerate. If you were brought up religious you can try not to be, or you can replace your old friends with new ones in a new part of the country, or leave the country altogether, as one of Avi's friends did—Amos, who moved to Paris and stayed, and today lives near the Canal Saint-Martin, and whose Hebrew sometimes has the sound of French in it. You could jump off the battered ocean liner of Jewish history altogether and swim for a different shore. You usually find out that who you are is not quite as malleable as you thought, but for a while you're intoxicated by the fluidity of things.

Avi's life in Tel Aviv was the first new version of himself that he had chosen but not the last. He was only twenty-one and still a soldier. Ireland was waiting. There were thousands of people still to talk to on buses, in bars, on the street, all over the world. When he bought a motorcycle the girls were surprised. They thought it was too dangerous, too dramatic a step for someone who was not even a civilian yet. "The world is spread out at my feet," he replied. He was restless. Every moment off the hill had to be exploited. "I'm bored," he would say, so the three of them would go out to a club or a restaurant, and after a while Avi would look at them and say, "I'm bored." Sometimes the girls arrived home to find that Avi had been there, released by some military whim, that he had showered and eaten and disappeared again, leaving behind oddly punctuated notes:

Girls: I was here, I enjoyed myself as usual (?) etc. etc. . . .

They left him notes of their own:

Avi
    Please—don't touch the books. I mean I need them just as they are.

Books weren't safe around him.

After these visits he pulled on his green pants and shirt, shouldered his rifle, and boarded a northbound bus out of the metropolis, toward the border and away from his new realm of freedom and clubs and girls, past the power station at Hadera, its three smokestacks perpendicular to the steely sheet of the winter sea, past the Arab town called the Mother of Coal, through the old kibbutz country of the Jezreel Valley to the Finger of Galilee. Then up the Hula Valley, past the Canaanite ruins of Hatzor, to the military airstrip serving the outposts of the security zone.

# 20

THE BOMBS ON the roads inside Lebanon were becoming more lethal in those days. Hezbollah technicians were starting to use cell phone triggers and laser triggers and eventually introduced a new kind of apparatus, a "hollow-charge" bomb, which propelled a molten mass of copper with enough force to penetrate an armored vehicle. These were hidden inside plastic rocks that Israeli soldiers attributed to diabolically clever camouflage experts but which were, according to one of the Hezbollah leaders, bought for fifteen dollars at stores selling garden ornaments. In order to avoid the roads the army decided to fly the Lebanon garrisons in on helicopters.

Avi arrived at the air base with one of the paperbacks his mother bought him every time he came home and with a bag of hamburgers from a nearby fast-food restaurant for his friends at the Pumpkin. This was a tradition. A giant helicopter waited on the tarmac with rotors drooping, the fuselage the size of a bus, its viability as an aircraft impossible to conceive when it was static. Before dusk the people in charge made lists of the soldiers, the helicopter lowered its ramp, and the men walked up in two straight lines like the convent-school girls from *Madeline*. They sat down on benches bolted to the sides and faced each other over crates.

After dark the engines barked, growled, and thundered to life. The men's nostrils filled with petrol fumes. The helicopter shook and lurched into the air, the passengers' stomachs dropped, and through the open ramp in the rear they saw the airfield and control tower fall away. The pilot flew north and kept the aircraft low, the dark hills walling the valley moving past on either side. The faces of the soldiers were barely illuminated by the weak cabin lights.

The pilot hugged the Lebanese hills and valleys and when he arrived under the Ali Taher ridge sent the aircraft rocketing upward until it was nearly level with the outpost. The behemoth touched down. The soldiers looked through the opening in the rear and saw a wild cloud of dust, soldiers with guns and fluorescent light sticks securing the landing pad and others with backpacks waiting in two rows to be taken home. The engine was so loud you couldn't make yourself heard even if you screamed. Avi ran out into the rotor blast and then up to the outpost, and a minute or two later the helicopter was thumping away into the darkness toward Israel and the hill was quiet. He was back.

With their service drawing to a close, the men who had been thrown together with Avi in that yard in the desert nearly three years before were no longer functioning as a platoon but had been scattered. Some were doing safe jobs inside Israel. One was an officer and had his own platoon. A few, including Avi, were in charge of running the Pumpkin's war room, keeping in touch with the detachment at Beaufort Castle, with headquarters down in Israel and with the teams that ventured out of the outpost into the countryside. When the Buttercup radar warned of an incoming shell it was the guys in the war room who got the message and intoned "Launch, launch" into the loudspeaker, always with the laconic tone of the unimpressed, and it was like touching a live wire to the outpost—everyone jumped and scrambled for cover. Where else would your words ever have such an effect?

Avi's old friend Gal, the Angel, manned the radios with him. By this time Avi was so broken-dicked that sometimes he put his head on Gal's shoulder and just left it there, eyes closed, and Gal embraced him until Avi found the strength to move again. It was his fourth tour at the Pumpkin. Each time was harder. Life was happening somewhere else without him. This was before many people were questioning the war in the security zone, but Avi didn't understand what the army was doing in Lebanon or what he was doing in the army. And yet a few months earlier a doctor had found a medical problem, a spinal cord defect, that could have been Avi's ticket to a desk job. The rebel A. wouldn't take it. He returned to the line.

He played chess with the outpost's Russian-born doctor. It was the first time, Avi announced, that he had met someone who was both an officer and intelligent. He argued with another soldier about the meaning of beauty, and told him: Take a silver cup, fill it with pomegranate seeds, and place it between the sunlight and the shade—that's beauty. It was a quote from the Talmud. He was kind to people he liked. When a tank officer, Mordechai, got stuck on the hill and ran out of clean underwear, Avi lent him a pair and never got them back. Mordechai, who will appear here again, had them for years.

With Gal he discussed Romain Gary's *The Kites*. One part that Avi loved was when the hero's old French teacher admits that he once dreamed of being a writer but that only one of his creative projects had ever succeeded—his wife. He had spent the fifty years of their

marriage inventing and reinventing her, and she him. This was the secret of their long happiness. The teacher thought anything not chiefly
the product of your imagination wasn't worth living with.

The carnal energies at the Pumpkin were highly concentrated;
the mere sound of a girl's voice coming over the radio at night from
Israel would cause a collective clenching of male throats across the
security zone. If the army had contrived a way to harness frustrated
sex drives to power the outpost, the soldiers would have been spared
the racket of the petrol generator, and if Hezbollah's technicians had
devised a scope that could somehow render visible what the guards
were seeing when they looked out into the darkness, the guerrillas
peering from the bushes would have been presented with an outpost
surrounded by ghostly breasts, floating nudes extending hands with
fingers folded inward to stroke a cheek. Avi was thinking about love
and reached a conclusion that wasn't original but brought him some
satisfaction: love was the best you could hope to achieve, and if you
found that the rest would work out. He wrote this in a letter to
Smadar and said the same thing to his mother in one of the conversations he and Raya had begun having in a cafe when he visited. He
wanted to fall in love, to lose control, to stop thinking so much for
a while.

# 21

WHEN AVI ARRIVED at the airstrip for his last flight up, the north of Israel was covered with rain clouds. The fields were turning to mud, and the outposts on some of the higher Lebanese peaks reported snow. The air force wouldn't fly. Avi went to his parents' home to spend the night. It was the beginning of February 1997. In less than a month the army would release him and his three-year trial would be over.

The next day he set out again into the storm. On the way he met one of his friends from the old platoon—Gil, who was now an officer. They stopped to buy hamburgers to take up to the hill and arrived late at the airstrip. The officer in charge was furious and said they wouldn't be allowed to board. But when that decision was communicated to the Pumpkin the outpost commander protested because he was short of men and no one could be spared. The officer at the airstrip relented and added them to the handwritten passenger list.

It was still raining, and the outposts in Lebanon were reporting strong winds and fog. There was talk of another postponement. Avi waited. When the air force finally approved the flight he took his gear and followed the others into a helicopter with the number 903 stenciled in yellow on the olive skin of the hull. His backpack rested on the floor near his boots. Inside the pack he had clean socks, fatigues, and a few books, including something by Gary: *The Life Before Us*, about the devotion of an Arab orphan to the retired Jewish prostitute who raised him.

In the cockpit the two pilots ran through their final checks. The same was happening inside a second helicopter parked nearby and headed to Beaufort Castle. On board the Beaufort helicopter was a team from a sister company of the Fighting Pioneer Youth, the brigade's antitank unit. The antitank unit isn't yet at the center of this story, but you should know that this team was missing one soldier, a stocky, bespectacled, and stubborn kid named Harel, which means "mountain of God." He had volunteered to become an officer and had recently departed for the army's command school in the desert. Also on this helicopter were tank crewmen, lookouts, and two trackers, Kamel and Hussein, cousins from the el-Heib Bedouin of Galilee.

In the dim light of Avi's helicopter were two faces he had known since the first day at the training base: Gil, the officer, and Shiloh, a quiet kid from one of the settlements in Samaria, who never quite fit in because he refused to become a cynic. Nearby was Avner, known by his family name, Alter, a star basketball player from a Jordan Valley kibbutz, who had been part of the rescue team at the Falcon Bend and was so seized by grief upon encountering the body of a friend that he flicked open his safety catch and fired at nothing at all until one of the officers calmed him down; Tom, raised in an experimental community built by Jews and Arabs who wanted to live together;

a popular lieutenant whose family had brought the Arabic name Abukassis with them from the Jewish quarters of North Africa; Vitaly, a cook from Baku; Mulatu, whose family lost nine members in the trek to Israel from Ethiopia five years earlier. A former Red Army medic from Kiev, Vadim, who came to Israel with the Soviet collapse and was now a reservist doctor, was seated on one of the benches. There were seventy-three men on board the two helicopters, and I realize while writing this that when I think of my country I'm thinking of them.

They lifted off at 6:48 p.m. On the radio Avi's helicopter was called Courier, and the other Chisel.

"Courier and Chisel are heading north," one of the pilots told the control tower.

One minute later, Avi's pilot requested permission to enter Lebanon. The code word for crossing the border was *omelet*, because the Hebrew word for "omelet," *havita*, is similar to the word for "crossing," *hatziya*.

"Courier and Chisel, omelet," the pilot of Avi's helicopter said into the receiver.

"Roger, omelet," said the air traffic controller.

"Permission for omelet," said the pilot again.

"Hold on," said the controller. In the back with the infantry the thunder of the engines drowned out anything but your thoughts, and no one heard any of this. Avi and the others knew only that they were airborne. As they waited for the controller, the pilots set off on a wide clockwise circle over the dark fields in the valley.

At 6:52 p.m. the pilot of Avi's helicopter radioed Gal, the Angel, who was in the war room up on the hill. Gal confirmed that the garrison was ready. The soldiers who were supposed to fly home were packed up and waiting.

Four minutes later the controller was on the frequency again. "Do you have contact with the land forces?" he asked the pilots. They did. Two minutes after that, the controller finally cleared them to enter the security zone.

One of the pilots said, "We're crossing over."

The helicopters were still above Israel. A night watchman at a cluster of fish ponds heard them coming. He was near the little cemetery of Kibbutz Dafna, an enclosure of old cypress and eucalyptus trees populated by founding pioneers, babies who didn't survive infancy, a pilot killed when his trainer plane crashed into the Sea of Galilee in 1962, a refugee who made it from Europe to the kibbutz in 1948 and died defending it a few months later.

The watchman looked up and saw the two black shapes pass overhead under the pale cloud ceiling. One was flying to the left and ahead of the other, but he saw them moving closer.

The rotors of the Beaufort-bound helicopter sliced into the bottom of Avi's helicopter, shearing off the ramp in the rear and sending it spinning into the night. Avi's backpack flew out and landed far below in one of the tributaries of the river Dan, where *The Life Before Us* was later recovered, muddy but legible. The second helicopter, without rotors, was now a metal box full of human beings six hundred feet in the air. It dropped next to the cemetery and exploded.

Avi's helicopter was damaged but still flying.

The pilot found himself over one of the villages in the valley. He switched on the landing lights, looking for a place to set down. But then the back of the helicopter broke off. Without its rear rotor the stricken aircraft began to spin as it fell, still hundreds of feet above the ground—once, twice, three times, the force of the rotation so powerful it tore benches from the cabin and threw Avi into the sky.

# Part Two

# 22

THE DAY AFTER the two helicopters crashed, while the country was trying to get used to the number seventy-three, no survivors, they took someone from Avi's company to a room in Tel Aviv where the army had the coffins laid out in rows. They asked him to identify the guys inside, his friends. When they opened the lids he saw—well, he saw Israel's secret weapon, because it has never been in a Mossad basement or in the vaults at Dimona, it was right there, in rows.

Dead young men are an important group in Israel, maybe the most important group. Their funerals are rites of passage: a sunny graveyard, a military cantor and an honor guard, parents who look like yours, girls crying behind sunglasses as they learn something they will spend years as wives and mothers trying to forget.

There is a culture that surrounds the dead: memorial books with photographs and letters, memorial evenings with songs and poems, a solemn tone of speech, short biographical movies with piano sound tracks that are shown every year on TV on Remembrance Day. That's the day when a siren sounds across the country and everything stops in honor of the dead soldiers—cars pull over on the highway, shoppers stand at attention in malls, clerks in their offices, five-year-olds in their kindergartens. Across the country there are hiking trails, groves of trees, lookout points and picnic areas named for the dead; you can be anywhere and suddenly come upon a stone marker engraved with the name of some young person. The stone is the common local limestone, which itself is made of bodies—microscopic creatures who died in the light zone at the surface of a prehistoric ocean and floated down through the darkness to the sea floor which is now our country, becoming the material that people here have always used to build their temples and homes.

In a field in northern Israel are seventy-three pieces of rough limestone arrayed around a circular pool. They are approximately human in size. If you visit at night you see that each is lit faintly from below, giving the stone a kind of illusory life. The impression is overpowering and unsettling, as if the men from those helicopters are standing silently around you, including you in their number, looking at the pool where their names are inscribed—Tom, Vadim, Alter, Abukassis, the rest. Among the names is Avi Ofner.

There are many layers of dead in this country. Take, for example, a day spent writing this book in my Jerusalem neighborhood. I sometimes stop working and run along a promenade that looks north over the city. At one end of the promenade is a marker informing passersby that fourteen men of the Jerusalem Brigade died here fighting the Egyptians in 1948 and another twenty fighting the Jordanians in 1967. If you read the lists you find that a man named Yosef Levi died both times. From that spot you can see across to the Mount of Olives, covered with the graves of 150,000 Jews buried over the millennia to be closest to the Temple Mount and the resurrection at the end of days.

Each time I walk to the neighborhood cafe where I write sometimes, I pass a neat plot of grass and rosemary bushes with two stone
markers inscribed "1914–1918." This is the mass grave of Indian soldiers who died fighting for the British against the Turks a century
ago. The markers bear the defunct ranks and units of Britain's Indian Army and the names of men whose lives ended far from home:
Afzal Hussein Shah, a sepoy in the 124th Duchess of Connaught's
Own Baluchistan Infantry; Chulam Muhammad, a lance naik of the
1/151st Sikh Infantry; Gunner Bur Singh of the Hong Kong Singa-
pore Mountain Battery. There are others who had safer jobs at camp
but died here anyway: Shoeing Smith Alam Idin of the Mule Corps;
Kneader Mansub Ali; a menial Bearer with just one name, Kolova.
Their faces and motivations lost to time, they now spend eternity
among apartments faced with limestone on a quiet street traveled
by Jewish schoolchildren with oversized backpacks, by parents with
strollers, and every fifteen minutes or so, by our local bus, the Number 7. Sometimes it feels as if the unusually spirited life of this country is playing out in a cemetery.

There is a special language used to describe our dead soldiers, a
language that makes them all sound the same, not just because you
can't say anything bad but because most were so young that there isn't
much to say at all. What they really were was potential. So in this
language they are always serious students, or mischievous ones, and
loving siblings, and good at basketball, and there was a funny thing
they did once on a class trip, and in the army they always helped their
friends. And they are, forever, "soldiers," though most thought they
were just doing that for a while before their real life resumed. It is said
in their honor that they were prepared to sacrifice themselves for the

rest of us, but of course they weren't, not most—they just thought it wouldn't happen to them, and the lucky ones weren't given time to realize they were wrong.

In all the years of the security zone no unit in the army was hit as hard as the engineering company of the Fighting Pioneer Youth. The soldiers who were left after the Falcon Incident and the helicopter crash had seen a third of their number vanish in nine months. Everyone knew Lebanon wasn't a real war, but those were real war losses.

*Avi (right) at the Pumpkin*

# 23

Now it's clear that February 4, 1997, the date of the helicopter accident in the Finger of Galilee, was the beginning of the end. This was when the security zone began to collapse under the weight of its contradictions. The way this happened had a lot to do with a small group of angry mothers.

I mentioned a soldier on Avi's helicopter known by his last name, Alter, a basketball player from Kibbutz Ashdot Yaakov. That kibbutz was one of the country's most successful communal farms before a feud in the 1950s between Stalinists and moderate socialists tore it into two separate communes right next to each other, both called Kibbutz Ashdot Yaakov, a fence between them. By the time Alter was growing up no one could really remember what it all had been about. One of Alter's favorite songs was the Hebrew ballad "Children of Winter '73," which has kids born after the Yom Kippur War chastising their parents for promising them peace and failing to deliver. Actually no one promised anyone anything, but it's still a popular song, and a line from it is engraved on Alter's tombstone. When you see it there what stands out isn't the text but that number, 73.

On the night of February 4 news of the crash reached one of the kibbutz members, a woman named Bruria, in the middle of a movie. Bruria's father was once the kibbutz librarian, and today she is the librarian. She has hair dyed eggplant purple and gets around on an old bike, both of these in keeping with the kibbutz style—style being one of the few things left of the kibbutz, the ideas having lived a remarkable life before dying a natural death, that beautiful experiment in radical egalitarianism played out, its presence at the heart of our society sorely missed and irreplaceable.

No one knew exactly what happened at first, but they were saying one of the Alter kids was en route to the Pumpkin and hadn't called. Bruria had been through a few wars. Her husband was wounded fighting the Syrians in 1973. She knew what it meant when officers in dress uniform arrived at the kibbutz gate, which happened five times in the 1973 war alone. But she trusted the country's leaders and accepted, as everyone did, that in Lebanon every year two dozen soldiers or so would be "sacrificed to the Molech," in her words, to protect the border. She had never questioned any of it. This time was different. She couldn't move on as she always had.

The grief from the Lebanon fighting was individual, usually not more than one or two soldiers at a time. Here an ambush, there a roadside bomb. One or two families would drop through the thin crust dividing our everyday lives here from the lava beneath the surface and climb back out disfigured by scars no one else could see, and things would go on. But seventy-three at once was different. This is a small country where people know each other. Everyone seemed to have someone on the helicopters. The crash was described at the time as an atom bomb, the release of a destructive force compared to which the insignificance of the cause—a series of arbitrary mishaps one evening in northern Israel—seems absurd.

For anyone looking at the war in the security zone, the helicopter crash is the *hijrah*, the point from which time is measured. Things happened either before or after. That the crash turned out to be the hinge around which the whole period revolved is an irony worth noting, because though later everyone came to accept Hezbollah's claim to be responsible for breaking our will and pushing us from Lebanon, if we are all being honest more credit is due to our air force. People have chosen to accept the enemy's narrative because that is easier than remembering that the worst wound in all the years of the Lebanon fighting, the decisive blow, was self-inflicted—a self-inflicted wound to end a self-inflicted war.

# 24

A FEW WEEKS after the crash Bruria saw an article in one of the kibbutz newspapers with the headline "Mothers in the Service of the Military." Israeli mothers, the writer charged, were sending their sons to die in the army for no reason. "How can we explain why maternal instincts work at full force only until the gate of the army induction center?" he wrote. "And how can we explain why for decades Israeli mothers have been crying afterwards and not lifting a finger beforehand?"

What moved Bruria even more than the text was the illustration: a drawing of a mother pushing a baby stroller that had tank treads for wheels. Mothers were preparing their boys for war from the cradle. They were creating wars by raising soldiers. If they stopped the wars would stop. It was the 1990s, and this is the way a lot of people were thinking. We didn't need to fight. Instead we could reason and withdraw our way out of our predicament. To a rational and optimistic person it made sense, and you can see the appeal even now: it meant not only that war was temporary, but that we were in control.

The reason for outposts like the Pumpkin was to keep the guerrillas from the border. But after the crash a few people started thinking in earnest that the security zone might be killing more people than it was saving, that the war there was unwinnable, and that we would solve the problem by leaving. They started thinking the army might be wrong.

Today that writer's call for mothers to stop the war reads like a crude appeal to sentiment, but in that hopeful decade of the new Middle East, and especially in the shock of the helicopter crash, it had power. To Bruria it seemed urgent. This was not just because one of the Alter kids was dead and other kibbutz kids were on the line, but because her own youngest son, Ofer, had just been drafted and was headed for Lebanon too. Later Ofer became one of the symbols of that time, and I'll mention him again.

# 25

THREE WEEKS AFTER the crash, when the Lebanon enterprise began to disintegrate—this was when the hill sought me out and began to insinuate itself into my life until my arrival there became inevitable. So it seems to me now. I was nineteen. I had been in the country since finishing high school in Toronto a year and a half before. I was in possession of a draft notice telling me to report that summer, so I knew it was my last civilian winter, though I didn't yet know what the military planned for me. I had the vague idea that I might spend a few quiet years in Israel's small navy, sailing back and forth in the Mediterranean.

I was on a bus in a Jerusalem of low skies and wet sidewalks. The radio was on, the announcer saying something about a battle in Lebanon. It involved a tank and a place with a funny name. I knew about the helicopters, of course, but the names of the outposts where they were headed hadn't made an impression, if I heard them at all. The radio broadcast on the bus was the first time I remember hearing of a hill called the Pumpkin.

What held my attention at that moment wasn't that name, or the name of the soldier who was dead, according to the announcer, but the name of an officer who was badly wounded, maybe dying—it was my friend Mordechai, whose unusually vigorous energies and curiosities I had encountered at the kibbutz where I worked as a hand in the dairy barn. This was a religious kibbutz atop Mount Gilboa in northern Israel, home to a small seminary that attracted unconventional high-school graduates not in a hurry to be drafted. Mordechai was enrolled there but often found his way out of the study hall to help with the cows. He disappeared into the Armored Corps soon after, and I had only the faintest idea what he was doing.

After the announcer said his name I looked around the bus, wondering if this could possibly be true. Much of me was still in the orderly Canadian city where I was born and grew up and where such things didn't happen. The other passengers looked straight ahead or out the window. Everything seemed normal.

A week later I traveled north with a friend, Jonah, who knew Mordechai too. We went to the hospital in Haifa and were in the corridor when a nurse passed going the other way, pushing a skeletal old man hunched in a wheelchair. I paid the man no mind until he lifted his right hand from the armrest, barely, and said my name, and it was him—bloodied, crippled, twenty-one years old, with the grin of a corpse.

In those dark days on the hill in February 1997, the weeks after the crash, it sometimes seemed to the men as if Avi and the others were just home on leave and would show up soon. Sometimes they couldn't remember who was still alive. They wrote the names of the dead on one of the walls. They thought fate must be done with them, but one night three weeks after the accident they spotted figures moving in the grass north of the outpost, and more moving under the ridge to the west—the guerrillas were coming up the riverbeds. Mordechai commanded one of the tanks. He and the three members of his crew pulled on their helmets and thundered down the hill.

Mordechai had his torso out of one of the hatches atop the turret, but he couldn't see anyone. The radio in his helmet crackled and a voice said, "They're on top of you."

He saw a flash from his left and ducked as a rocket mangled one of his machine guns. Three figures moved behind a clump of boulders, and the gunner swiveled the cannon and fired. Looking in the tank's thermal sight, which is designed to see tanks at night from afar, the gunner saw a human shape that filled the screen. He fired again. A person is not substantial enough to cause a tank shell to explode, so the shell went right through, but that was enough.

Lior, the loader-radioman, handed Mordechai grenades, and Mordechai ripped out the pins and threw them from the turret. The driver shouted that there was someone in front of the tank, and he forced the gas pedal down—in the video filmed from the lookout post that night, all in shades of green, you see seventy tons of steel pounce and a small figure disappear under the treads.

Mordechai wore olive drab coveralls, a flak jacket, fireproof gloves, and black boots. Underneath he had on long underwear, a white undershirt, and two pairs of gray socks. He wore dog tags. In his pocket was a knitted skullcap. In a box behind him were wafers, pretzels, chips, chocolate, and black coffee. His rifle was on the turret along with four clips and two canteens. In another pocket of his coveralls, inside a plastic pouch, he had a mystical book the size of a matchbox written in minuscule Hebrew letters. It was called *The*

*Book of the Angel Raziel.* Mordechai's mother had given it to him because she thought it might protect him from harm.

The army found four bodies afterward. They were around Mordechai's age. They had rifles, ammunition clips, grenades, food, candy, and gum. They had a Russian missile launcher. One had a photograph of the ayatollah Khomeini. Another had a video camera. They wore red-and-green headbands, camouflage coats, and dog tags, and in their packs were worry beads. Each had a small Qur'an.

When everything was quiet again Mordechai brought his tank back to the outpost. The crew replenished the ammunition and made sure the tank was ready for more, just in case. Inside the cramped interior the four of them tried to figure out exactly what happened. They were giddy. Mordechai explained to Lior that there was a prayer of thanksgiving recited upon surviving danger: "Blessed are you, Lord, our God, King of the Universe, who bestows kindness upon the undeserving, who has bestowed kindness upon me." It did seem for a while that they had survived.

Just before dawn the radio crackled again. The lookouts at the Pumpkin spotted someone crawling where the bodies of the guerrillas lay in the grass. The tank raced over. The sky was gray by this time, and Mordechai saw the lights in Nabatieh going off. Lior emerged from the belly through one of the hatches to look out for missiles. It was 5:57 a.m. The tank stood still for a moment, dull green metal on the deep green slope, two torsos and helmeted heads jutting from the circular openings on the turret—Mordechai and Lior.

A missile hit the tank; Mordechai heard himself screaming from afar and saw the scene as if from above; he dropped inside, passed out, and came to when the gunner stepped on him; Mordechai's face was wet with blood and he couldn't see with his left eye; his left arm seemed to be gone at first, but turned out to be attached by a strand of muscle. He kept his wits. He got the tank back to the outpost. The crew received a medal for all of this later.

Mordechai even got himself out and stood on his feet as the medics ran up. One of them was Gal, the Angel. When they grabbed Mordechai, taking care with his arm, he was asking about Lior—what about Lior? Someone said not to worry because Lior was fine. That wasn't true, he was dead at nineteen inside the tank, but you can't blame anyone for lying.

In the hospital Jonah and I couldn't quite picture what happened, or the place where it happened. Mordechai appeared to us like an explorer returned from a world unreachable from our own.

In Mordechai's dreams about the battle afterward, he was always an infantryman for some reason, always running among the boulders, never a tank officer. He doesn't know why. He was sure at first that if he had been a better officer Lior would still be alive—if he had positioned the tank differently, if, if. Once his body healed everything else began to crack, the course of his life derailed, and he found himself in a black hole for which the psychiatrists have many names and medications. It has taken him years to climb out. A different man would not have climbed out. Today he treats people who have suffered head injuries. The proximity of the edge is still very much on his mind.

I visited him one night not long ago in Jerusalem. His wife was out. We talked quietly by the door to his dark kitchen, his four children asleep in the next room, a tiny fragment of his tank still embedded in his left eye.

# 26

NOT LONG AFTER we visited Mordechai in the hospital, Jonah ended up in Mordechai's old outfit. When a loader-radioman in a crew bound for the Pumpkin made the reasonable decision that he wasn't going, and disappeared, the unit sent Jonah as a replacement.

During his time in the army Jonah spent many hours memorizing poetry to stave off boredom. He started with a pocket paperback of Natan Alterman's *Stars Outside* and still remembers fragments:

> . . . *the city bathed in the cries of crickets*
> . . . *the moon on the cypress bayonet*
> . . . *I will not stop looking, and I will not stop breathing,*
>        *And I will die and keep walking*

When he had committed the whole volume to memory he found some cheap English classics at a Jerusalem bookstore and picked up a Poe collection that included "The Raven." He learned to recite it off by heart and still can. English wasn't a problem for him because he was born in Toronto, like me—we were friends as children before his family moved to Israel years before mine did the same.

Jonah's crew would head out of the outpost most nights on an enterprise known as an Artichoke ambush, so named because you were supposed to use the tank's night sight, the Artichoke, to spot guerrillas and then kill them with the cannon from afar. It was hard to imagine bad things happening during an activity named for an artichoke, but they did with some regularity, sometimes to our enemies and sometimes to us.

The four crewmen took turns standing guard in the turret in case guerrillas crept through the bushes up to the tank. The others dozed inside. Sometimes a voice came from the radio and it would be the war room at the Pumpkin or some other outpost, or a girl down in Israel if you were lucky, and you would be reminded of the existence of other people on earth. But most of the time it was quiet. It was quiet that night too, and cold, with just enough wind to chill your bones but not enough to blow away the fog. Jonah scanned the bushes with night goggles and was taking it seriously, because some thought nothing would ever happen but Jonah had seen what Mordechai looked like and knew better.

> Once upon a midnight dreary, while I pondered, weak and
>      weary
> Over many a quaint and curious volume of forgotten lore

Things were bad enough without Poe in the tank, but he recited it aloud anyway:

> Ah, distinctly I remember it was in the bleak December,
> And each separate dying ember wrought its ghost upon the
>      floor

Which was funny, because it happened just then to be a bleak December, and "Deep into that darkness peering, long I stood there wondering, fearing" was also pretty accurate, and by this time Jonah was spooked, but he kept reciting the poem as he moved his head back and forth, and that was when he heard a rustle next to the tank and saw the shape scuttling on the ground, and it was real, not his imagination, and his heart stopped and started racing at the same moment, like three heart attacks all at once, and it was a plastic bag. That is a real Pumpkin story, and I wanted to tell it here because I realize that isn't how most of my stories end, but it is how most ended in real life.

# 27

REPORTS BEGAN TO reach Bruria about people from nearby kibbutzim who were organizing in favor of a pullout from Lebanon. The nucleus was a group of four women who, like Bruria, had sons of army age. When the same reporter behind the first essay about the complicity of Israeli mothers interviewed them in the kibbutz newspaper two months after the crash, he called them the "four mothers," like the four matriarchs of Genesis. This was the birth of the Four Mothers movement. It didn't look like much at first.

When Bruria heard that the women would be standing one Friday holding signs at an intersection, she decided to join them. A half-dozen women came, and a few photographers. Some drivers cursed them as they passed, because at this time most people still believed that without the security zone the north of Israel would be in danger, and if you opposed the army many thought you were a traitor. The mothers didn't oppose the army, just the policy, but it was hard to make that clear. There was bad blood in the country at the time over the peace negotiations with the Palestinians, and people assumed that the mothers were from the left, which they were, though they didn't think the argument about Lebanon needed to break down along the old political lines. Bruria began writing down the curses in a little notebook, not that they were particularly imaginative, mostly "Go fuck Arafat," "Nasrallah's whores," etc., etc. Nasrallah was the secretary-general of Hezbollah.

Bruria was opinionated and tough, the way the kibbutz assembly line used to make them, and once the matter was clear to her she could not be budged. The security zone was not the solution to a problem. It was the problem. The helicopter crash was an accident, but it had thrown the strategy into relief. Why were soldiers flying in helicopters? Because they were threatened by bombs on the roads. Why were the soldiers on the roads? Because they were traveling to a line of isolated forts in an enemy country. And why were they in these forts? No one seemed to have asked that question for a long time.

Bruria researched the history of the security zone and found that not only had it not been seriously debated by the government in years, but there had never quite been a decision to create it in the first place. The wording of the relevant government resolution from 1984, two years after the invasion, called for the complete withdrawal of the army from Lebanon and the establishment of a buffer zone along the border that would be controlled by the South Lebanon Army, the Christian militia allied with Israel, "with the support of the Israel Defense Forces." But the army never withdrew. And that tiny fragment of language, "with the support of the Israel Defense Forces"—in Hebrew, only two words—had led over years of creeping "support" to the Pumpkin, Beaufort Castle, convoys, ambushes, the whole landscape that became the center of the universe for so many of us, a war so long that kids who were toddlers when it started fought there when they grew up.

The security zone had come to be seen not as a decision anyone made but as a state of nature. That's why this war never had a name—a name would suggest a decision. Instead it was referred to simply as Lebanon. It was something that just existed and always would. This wasn't a matter of debate as long as the price wasn't too high. But the helicopter crash made the price too high, and that spring Bruria and a few others resolved that if no one had the courage to end it they would end it themselves.

# 28

ONE DAY LATE that summer mortars hit the Pumpkin. Reports of a flower went out over the radio and were soon updated to oleander. It was one of the platoon leaders. Down in Israel, the gentle women of the army's grim notification machinery picked up phones. A car with a few officers moved through suburban streets. The news dropped like a boulder into a still pond: parents, siblings, girlfriend, friends. Later that day the information reached the training base of the Fighting Pioneer Youth at the encampment by the desert highway, then made its way to a sergeant in charge of the twenty recruits beginning their three years of service in the brigade's antitank company, one of them me.

The sergeant called one of the new kids aside. It was Dani, for whom army service was a step on the way from a middle-class childhood to a doctorate on the modern history of Lebanon, a hiatus spent as a medic training to save lives and dreading the possibility of actually being called upon to do so. Just then we were standing in three rows trying with desperate ineptitude, and under threat of punishment, to precisely line up the toes of our new red boots in accordance with an order from the sergeants. But the discipline was abruptly relaxed, the first time this had happened, and no one was sure what to do. Boots began to stray from the line. There was bad news about someone Dani knew from home. A hill in Lebanon, a mortar shell. We all saw him start to cry, and there was the Pumpkin again.

Not long after that our platoon was convened in a classroom to hear a war story told by a slight sergeant. It was Yaacov, from the incident at the Falcon Bend the year before. He was now at the desert base training the two dozen men of the engineering company's new draft—this was a sister platoon, housed in tents next to ours. They were with us in the classroom. Anytime we were allowed to sit down our heads dropped and we fell asleep, but this didn't happen when he told us about that night. It was a gripping story, an awful story with no virtue to redeem it, and I think it was meant as a first warning about our future beyond the training base. The outpost's name was familiar to me by now.

The engineering company had always been in charge of the Pumpkin, so at first we looked at those recruits with a mix of pity and envy; our unit had a less perilous assignment. The engineers were on their knees that summer, and everyone knew they were cursed.

While we were still in basic training someone high up decided the engineering company had suffered enough and that our company had not. Papers moved around in an office somewhere; a document was signed by a distracted officer, stamped, filed by a clerk, fates thus decided. The engineers were moved off the hill to a part of the security zone that was supposed to be safer. There, near the border fence one night, an officer triggered a booby trap with his radioman, and both of them died.

# 29

WITH THE PASSION of the new proselyte, Bruria approached drivers at intersections and shoved the Four Mothers petition through the windows of their cars. She pounced on unsuspecting visitors to the kibbutz library. She had a button that said GET OUT OF LEBANON IN PEACE, blue letters on a white background, and wore it everywhere. There are pictures from her daughter's wedding where you see it pinned to her dress. Things in Lebanon seemed to be getting worse. Nearly one hundred soldiers died that year, 1997, in and around the security zone: the helicopter crash, a squad of commandos who walked into a Hezbollah ambush along the coast, five infantrymen trapped and incinerated when a shell lit a brush fire, a steady drip of others.

The women posted their manifestos on kibbutz bulletin boards and used their connections to get important people to meet them. Few took them seriously. The government ignored them, and public opinion was somnolent. It was common to hear said, by men of course, that the mothers were "speaking from the uterus." Bruria tried hard not to say where she thought the men were speaking from.

In the fall of that same year something else happened on Bruria's kibbutz.

There was another member, Orna, who was the former manager of the communal factory and the incarnation of a giant piece of earth-moving machinery in the body of a wiry woman with a shock of blond hair. Orna had her doubts about the wisdom of the security zone, but she didn't like protests at intersections. She also had a son, Eyal, her youngest, commanding a tank northeast of the Pumpkin, at the outpost called Basil. Protesting seemed like a betrayal.

Orna was living at the time with what she calls a "paralyzing fear" about her son. People who know Orna, and nearly everyone in the Jordan Valley does, know she is not a woman easily paralyzed. Orna had a brother who died in the air force long before. She was kibbutz secretary in 1973 when the army notification teams showed up those five times at the gate. She knew what it looked like: a taxi with a few officers in dress uniforms come to knock on a door and enact the secret ritual at the country's heart. She called them the "green angels of death." When her Eyal was born she named him for one of her friends, a kibbutz kid who died in the 1973 war.

Eyal was the same age as Alter, who died in the helicopter crash. They grew up together in the children's house, which meant they were more like siblings than friends. Eyal showed up late to Alter's funeral that February, armed and in uniform. He stood with the rest of the kibbutz and surprised his mother by bursting into tears. This was in the days of the debate about whether crying at funerals should be allowed, the real question being whether we're still strong enough to survive here. There were generals who said soldiers shouldn't cry, but it turned out not to be the kind of thing you can regulate.

Eyal believed in the mission in Lebanon. He thought the Four Mothers didn't know what they were talking about, which is what all of the soldiers thought at the time, if they thought about it at all. Orna and Bruria had known each other for decades, but Orna didn't sign her friend's petition.

Orna was in charge of gardening, and early one morning in September she was preparing one of the lawns for a kibbutz wedding. She had a Walkman clipped to her belt and listened to the radio through earphones as she worked. At 7 a.m. the announcer reported "heavy exchanges of fire" in Lebanon, which was the code. She kept working.

A few days before, Eyal had asked her to set up a meeting with the kibbutz secretary the next time he came home on leave. Members were debating in those days whether the kibbutz should be privatized, and though most of the young people were in favor, Eyal wanted the secretary to know he wasn't. He liked the kibbutz the way it was. Orna walked over to the secretary's office to make an appointment.

The receptionist had her back to the door. She didn't turn around, and Orna asked her what was wrong. Nothing, the receptionist said, in Orna's recollection, and she still didn't turn around. The kibbutz secretary opened the door to his office and saw Orna. He closed the door. She walked out and met her brother-in-law, whose son was at Beaufort Castle. The kibbutz had a half-dozen kids on the line. She asked him if there was news from the castle, and he said no.

Orna wasn't stupid. She knew something had happened to one of the kids, even if she didn't know what everyone else did—that it was hers, killed when a missile hit his tank at 6:25 a.m. She saw a taxi coming from the direction of the gate. In the back were figures in green. When the taxi passed the tennis court she finally understood what was about to happen to her and started running crazed across the pavement. She collapsed near the net. She doesn't remember much after that, only that when the green men reached her she was on the ground looking up, begging them to say he was just wounded.

# 30

THE NEXT DAY the whole kibbutz took the dirt road past the aqueduct built by members in 1938 to the little cemetery overlooking orchards along the Jordan. They buried her son near his namesake from the Yom Kippur War, and near his friend Alter.

It took Orna time to walk upright again. But when she could she joined forces with Bruria. She made the campaign to get the army out of Lebanon her reason for living. She turned out to have a knack for organization and for slogans. She was relentless.

Soon she was spending a month with a few other women outside the official residence of the president in Jerusalem, sitting on the sidewalk with a sign that read WE ARE DYING AND YOU ARE SILENT. She knew things were more complicated, but you needed to keep it simple. When she wrote *we* she meant her son and herself, because Orna wasn't sure she was still alive.

It was cold, and it rained. It was hard to sleep. For a while people were stopping to shout "Nasrallah's whores," the usual things. But by this time journalists were paying attention to the Four Mothers, especially women journalists—there were a few important ones who liked what the mothers were saying and had begun giving them airtime.

Orna did a radio interview on her cell phone one rainy evening, and when she looked up she saw a traffic jam; she remembers this as the moment she knew things had turned in their favor. There weren't many radio stations in Israel, and most of the drivers seemed to be listening to the interview and looking at her at the same time. They understood what had happened to her and what she was trying to say, or so she thought. She might have been wrong. But the curses stopped and what came instead were pizzas, dozens of pizzas, which people ordered to the tent or brought themselves. When someone asked Orna what they could do to help, what she needed, she said pizza. That's what she ate for a month until she decided the point had been made and went home.

At the Pumpkin around this time a tank crewman lost his legs in a barrage of mortars and rockets, and two infantrymen were sent into shellfire to look for them in the mud. They found one—a leg with a black boot, severed at the thigh. It was heavier than they expected.

# Part Three

# 31

THE BIG TRUCKS passed through fields lowing like cattle and moved north through the border gate, swift shepherd jeeps in the lead and rear. A few soldiers stood at the fence, no one we knew. They raised their hands as we left the country and swung the gate closed behind us.

Twenty riflemen sat on benches with weapons strapped diagonally across their torsos, barrels between their knees. Mine pointed down to a field radio, my radio, on the floor between two red boots, shifting and jumping with the movement of the truck. It was winter, early 1998, the rainy season, and Lebanon was lush and eerie—steep slopes, a lofty clump of cedars. The trucks descended into a valley in low gear, crossed a bridge, and then began to climb. There were bombs on the roads, we knew that. There were guerrillas in the bushes.

Harel was there in the truck—helmet, glasses, an impassive face, the "mountain of God," child of the helicopter crash. He was our platoon leader and had been since the day of our arrival at the training base eight months before. We still addressed him with trepidation and only when necessary. We had learned not long before that he was the only survivor from his platoon, that the seventy-three included all of his friends: a surgeon's son from Jerusalem; some kibbutzniks;

Alejandro, who was born in Argentina—the usual well-meaning kids who join units like ours, a whole team from the company to which we now belonged. Seventy-three. A year had passed, but the country hadn't recovered. We were going into Lebanon on a truck because the army was still afraid to fly us in.

Today Harel lives on Mount Gilboa, runs a cowshed in the valley, and has four black-haired boys as stubborn as he. I speak to him often, and he still doesn't say much.

Harel heard about the crash at the desert base where he was training to be an officer. He went to as many funerals as he could, finished the officers' course on schedule, and returned to the company in time to take charge of twenty recruits drafted out of high school that summer, us. We were his new platoon, and eventually I understood that we had been in the shadow of the helicopter crash from the day we first lined up in the yard and heard our names called, as when an old secret is revealed to you in adulthood and many things about your family become clear.

Once, in a television interview, Harel was asked how he did it—how he went back to the army after what happened. He looked at the interviewer for a moment. Here was a chance for an expression of ideology or faith, a love of country, all of those generations of Jews looking at him, depending on him not to give up. In the fighting in Jerusalem in 1967 some of the soldiers claim they felt King David himself pushing them through the alleyways. How did Harel go back? There might have been a flicker of disdain in his eyes, but otherwise he betrayed no emotion. "On the bus," he said. It is one of the great lines.

I arrived at the Pumpkin with a shouted command in the truck, a crush of packs and rifles, and a moment of air travel into mud. When I straightened my knees and lifted my head I saw a valley running toward a distant white-capped massif, the sky of a Levantine winter stretched like a great leaden tent over hills of emerald, olive, and jade. I'm not sure I had ever seen anything so beautiful. I was looking the wrong way.

Someone took my arm and spun me around, and under a helmet I recognized the company commander. He pointed uphill to a jumble of dun netting and concrete. The urgency of reaching the outpost before shells welcomed our convoy had been made clear to us, but I needed to be told again: *Run.*

We ran from the trucks into a courtyard ringed by high embankments and then through a tunnel into the safety of a bunker. I dropped my radio but kept my helmet on and tried to appear unruffled, as if I came to places like this all the time. There were guys from our company's other platoons on beds stacked three high on each side of a long room. We were the greenest of the soldiers who would hold the hill for the next four months. The lowest rung of the company's ladder was ours. The bunker's inhabitants gave us the disdainful stare of the battle-weary, and I remember believing they had acquired some profound knowledge of war that we lacked. They had arrived at the outpost for the first time a week before, the week was quiet, and they had spent most of it washing pots.

On one bed were boxes of junk food from home. On another, a television showed *Life of Brian* with Hebrew subtitles. The rough cement floor between the bunks was clean, with no bloodstains or any other hint of the wounded soldiers who had been treated lying there before they were helicoptered away.

Down the hill was an intersection where the steep access road to the Pumpkin joined the main road. Harel took a few of us to secure this spot while the convoy got out. We found the trucks lined up and growling, their engine grilles facing south, eager to be out of danger. After we flattened ourselves around the intersection, barrels pointing out into the foreign countryside, the first jeep sped off toward Israel, the rest of the convoy followed, and soon we were alone.

Ofir lay peering through his rifle scope at a clump of trees not far away; he is now a thirty-five-year-old shiatsu therapist, but was then an eighteen-year-old marksman. Harel crouched on the shoulder and I lay on my stomach beside him, straining my neck muscles against the weight of the helmet, the bulk of the radio on my back pressing my rib cage into the ground. It was hard to breathe. Here we were. But where was that?

It is hard to recall how little you once knew, and harder to admit it. I understood that we were Israeli soldiers; that our enemies were Arab fighters, whom we called terrorists, and that we should kill them before they killed us; that the battlefield was this place, Lebanon. I knew I couldn't let my friends down. That was it. Matters seemed fairly clear to me that first day.

Across a valley to the east, inside the security zone, I made out a town spread along the top of another ridge by the antenna of a military emplacement. Harel said this was Marj Ayoun, a Christian town with an Israeli base. I was aware in some imprecise way that there were Christians here and that they were our allies, but in the spare lines of my mental map of the Middle East in those days the place of Christians, Arabic-speaking Christians, was uncertain. Everything seemed ominous—the trees, the bushes, the strange town with its strange name. Ofir was saying something in an urgent whisper and motioning toward the valley without removing his eye from the rifle's scope. He saw two armed men.

Harel ran over in a crouch, and just then came the crack and dull echo of a gunshot. Some of us exchanged glances, not having expected things to unfold like this: minutes after our arrival, in daylight. Harel motioned me over with the radio. In the valley, perhaps three hundred yards away, I saw the two figures. They made no effort to conceal themselves. They walked casually and carried rifles. One of them raised his, and we heard another shot. Everyone ducked, though they weren't aiming at us. They're in civilian clothes, Ofir said.

Harel told him to put them in his sights, but of course they were already there, they were close to dying; it required a slight increase in pressure from the index finger of a disoriented teenager.

Harel took the old-fashioned telephone receiver attached to my radio by a long rubber coil, pressed the button on the side, and asked the outpost what to do. The outpost said we shouldn't do anything, because the two were probably just hunters, Christians from one of the villages. Harel stood up. *Ruh*, he shouted, which means "go away"—this is one of the Arabic words known to every Israeli soldier. The two stopped and looked in our direction. They stood for a moment and then sauntered off, pausing every so often to shoot at something we couldn't see, maybe pheasants. Soon they were gone, having planted in our minds some doubt about what, exactly, was going on.

Back at the outpost an officer appeared in the bunker and summoned me and one or two other newcomers. We followed him up concrete steps, emerged into the soft light of early evening, and found ourselves in a trench running around the Pumpkin along the top of the embankments. The officer called this the "fighting level." You entered the trench, we were told, wearing a helmet, flak jacket, and webbing, and with rifles loaded. The way was just wider than an infantryman in full gear, so to pass someone both of you had to turn sideways.

What followed after I stepped into the trench for the first time was a tour of a landscape that has not left me since: the sandbags stacked four or five high, and beyond them the Forest, and the hostile town below to the west, the hidden riverbeds rising toward us from its houses, the hilltops of our ridge rolling to the north, Beaufort Castle far to the south. We spent hours and days and months looking at the little world around the hill, doing nothing else, just looking. I have never known another place in the same way. Just as glare lingers after you close your eyes, so that view remains imprinted on my retinas years later.

The purpose of the tour was not to tell the outpost's stories or to explain the complexities of where we were and why. I was unaware of all that, and the officer guiding me certainly was too. I was barely twenty, and he not much older. There were no signs marking where bodies had lain the previous year or the one before—if you have read to this point, you know far more about the hill than any of us did then. The tour was meant only to introduce our new surroundings quickly, before we lost the light, so we could begin taking our turn in the guard posts.

# 32

THE NEXT MORNING someone came through the bunker and shook us awake for Readiness with Dawn. We emerged cursing from warm green cocoons into fluorescent light. Our uniforms and boots were never to come off, so we didn't have to put them on. Up in the trench, the first muezzin calls drifted up from Nabatieh and the sky grew light.

We had come anticipating "action," but after our arrival nothing happened. We were urged not to let our guard down because something would soon. Nabatieh, we were told, was a "nest of terrorists." Anyone moving within a few hundred yards of the outpost was to be shot, even someone who seemed harmless, like a shepherd with his flock; the shepherds were often Hezbollah scouts. The townspeople knew our rules and kept their distance. Even if you weren't sure what you saw was real, even if you were nearly certain it was just a bush or a shadow, you opened fire—those were the orders and had been since the guerrillas with their flag and video camera caught the Pumpkin unprepared three and a half years before. If any of the sentries began shooting, the entire garrison was to conclude that we were being attacked. Then everyone opened up with light machine guns, heavy machine guns, machine guns that fired grenades, whatever weapons were at hand; this made an impressive noise, if nothing else, and was known as a "crate of fire," another of the army's poetic flourishes.

Still nothing happened. On more than one occasion, a night sentry looking at the town saw a red light arcing toward him and shouted "incoming" into the radio only to see more lights—green, blue, yellow—rising into the sky and bursting apart as people in the nest of terrorists celebrated a wedding with fireworks.

Sometimes tank gunners peered at night into their thermal sights, which could pick up heat miles away, and saw figures moving in groups of three or four. Terrorists! No, wild boars, unfortunate creatures common in these parts, who liked to travel at night in small groups like guerrillas, and who looked human when seen from afar on a thermal sight. They knew unhappy years while nervous Israelis ruled their countryside, and many had their brief, hairy lives curtailed by our shells.

Some of the buildings in Nabatieh had names. There was one called Dir Mar Antonius, which was a garble to me at the time but which I later understood meant the Monastery of Saint Anthony, indicating the presence of Christians among the Shiites of the town. There was a hospital (al-Ghandour), a gas station (Cal-Tex), and many mosques. On the outskirts stood a row of damaged villas, abandoned because of our gunfire; Avi described one of them in a letter. At the time I didn't pay much thought to the word *abandoned*, which seemed like a straightforward description of houses, like "brick" or "square." I didn't consider what had led them to be abandoned or where their inhabitants were now.

The Red Villa was so called because it had red brick on its facade, and the White Villa had presumably been white, but now it was just a roof; after the guerrillas used it to fire rockets at the outpost some time before, an Israeli unit was sent over the Red Line to blow it up. The most memorable location was known to us as the House of Babes—I am cleaning up the Hebrew slightly, because the word is a dirtier one than *babe*. There is no English equivalent. The house was given its name because it was inhabited by a woman, just one, with dyed blonde hair. The field intelligence lookouts could see her with their binoculars and cameras. The Babe was not a guerrilla, obviously, just someone who used to leave in the morning and come back in the evening. Her appearances were celebrated; such was our deprivation. The lookouts had compiled a videotape of sightings.

# 33

Two men I never met, Thomas Dodd and Archibald Affleck, both happened to arrive in the British line in France the same year, 1916, the former with a battery of the Royal Field Artillery and the latter with one of the Canadian divisions. Thomas was from Chester, England, and Archie from the Ottawa Valley. Both survived.

A series of grand and modest events ended up linking them to me: the profound impact of their war on Europe and the Middle East, the upending in those years of the well-ordered world of their parents and grandparents and the brutalizing of the collective human mind, the collapse of the Hapsburg and Ottoman Empires, Lord Balfour's famous declaration of 1917 in favor of a "national home" for the Jews. And historical developments of a lesser order: the marriage during the next war of Archibald's son, a Canadian lieutenant who had survived the sinking of his Royal Navy corvette by a German mine, to Thomas's daughter, who followed her husband across the ocean from England to Toronto in 1945 and gave birth to a daughter of her own. And then the marriage of this daughter, my mother, to the son of two Jewish escapees from Eastern Europe—a milliner whose family was consumed by the Germans along the Bug River in

Poland in 1940 and a tailor who had fled the Russian advance at Lemberg in 1914 as a child. These events and others conspired to place me, the great-grandson of Thomas and Archie, in circumstances whose politics would have baffled them both but whose physical trappings would have been familiar. Members of our family watched the twentieth century begin and end from a sandbagged trench.

Even the language we spoke in Lebanon wouldn't have seemed entirely foreign to them, though neither is likely ever to have heard a word of Hebrew. We described our journey into the security zone as "going up to the line," for example, and our mission there as "holding" it. Some might recognize Readiness with Dawn as a descendant of the dawn stand-tos that made such an impression on the Great War poets, the same "highly ritualized distillation of the state of anxious stalemate," as Paul Fussell described it in *The Great War and Modern Memory*. I don't mean to suggest that our conflict was in a league with theirs, only to note the migration of words and genes and to point out what any student of middle-school chemistry knows, which is that things are made of odd pieces of older things.

Within a few years elements of the security zone war would, in turn, appear elsewhere and become familiar to everyone in the West: Muslim guerrillas operating in a failed and chaotic state; small clashes in which the key actor is not the general but the lieutenant or private; the use of a democracy's sensitivities, public opinion, and free press as weapons against it. In this kind of war events are so prolonged that no single soldier can see them the whole way through and so fragmentary it is hard to assemble a coherent history afterward. The old staff-history lingo of "flanking movements" and "divisional feints" becomes useless, and the relative rarity of death leaves time to focus on individuals in a way that sometimes makes death harder to bear. If my ancestors' great war was the first of the twentieth century, I believe our little one was the first of the twenty-first.

It was a week or two after our arrival that I finally heard a hiss in the air above my guard post. I didn't react because I always thought shells whistled. This was just a soft whisper in the sky, as if the universe was imparting a secret. In a way this was true: the secret, one familiar to Thomas and Archie, was that my continued existence on earth was now a matter of parabolas. The whisper built in volume before ending in a concussion that shook the hill, and then I understood and crouched under the parapet. "Launch, launch," said our loudspeaker, and the sky leaned toward me again and whispered something into my ear.

# 34

THAT SPRING A squad of religious soldiers appeared at the Pumpkin armed with blowtorches. They had been sent by the military rabbinate to prepare the outpost for the festival of Passover, when the consumption of bread is forbidden. The visitors worked furiously outside the outpost gate, in ill-fitting helmets and flak jackets issued for this rare trip into a combat zone, scouring all of our pots and cutlery against the backdrop of the Lebanese hills. They left behind crates of army matzah. The festive meal, the seder, is one of the most important events for Jewish families in Israel, and not being home for it was considered a great misfortune.

When the night of the festival arrived we sat on the triple-decker bunks, forty or fifty of us, the Bedouin trackers, everyone. One of the officers led us through the course of the seder, interrupted by messages coming from the war room and by the hourly rotation of the sentries. We followed along in army-issue copies of the *haggadah*, which contains the order of the meal and the texts read aloud by participants; I still have mine, hurriedly inscribed in ballpoint pen, *Outpost Pumpkin, Passover 1998*. One of the holiday foods is a paste made of apples, dates, and nuts called *haroset*, meant to evoke the mortar of the Israelite slaves in Egypt. It turned out the army had manufactured little silver vacuum packets with balls of the stuff, like astronaut food.

That was the best illustration I've experienced of how ritual can remind us who we are and keep us moving through the year no matter how extreme the circumstances. We were stranded on a hilltop beyond our borders. Not many of the soldiers observed religious law. It would have been entirely logical to skip the seder. And yet this wasn't even considered. It was obvious to us that we would have a seder, that matzah and *haroset* would appear, that soldiers would risk their lives on the convoy roads to clean the dishes. No one thought twice about it.

My sense of our place in the landscape was primitive in those days. I still thought of us as Israelis, as something new and foreign in the world I saw beyond the trench. I prayed sometimes with some others on the Sabbath and read lines like "The voice of the Lord breaks cedars, the Lord shatters the cedars of Lebanon," which is from Psalms. And from the Song of Songs we have

> With me from Lebanon, my bride
> Come with me from Lebanon
> Descend from Amana's peak
> From the peaks of Senir and Hermon
> From the dens of lions, from the hills of leopards

Once you begin looking for Lebanon in the Hebrew texts it's everywhere. So part of me must have understood the depth of the geographic connection even before I learned about the synagogues in Lebanese towns not far away, like Hamdoun and Tyre, abandoned with the exodus of the one million Jews of the Islamic world in my parents' lifetime. We weren't far from Aleppo, Syria, where just a few years before, in the early 1990s, the last Jews had shuttered a synagogue in use since Byzantine times. Most of these people remained in the Middle East, in Israel, and their children and grandchildren were with me in the trench. This was one of the things that made our situation different from that of an American soldier in Iraq.

I wouldn't want to give the impression that the Pumpkin was the scene of much thinking, though Israeli teenagers are more thoughtful than most, growing up as they do in a complicated place that demands their attention and forces them to assess their attitude toward it sooner or later, and faced early on with the awareness of grieving people and high stakes. On the hill at this time there was still no indication of the debate beginning to spread in Israel about whether we should be in Lebanon at all. There was a sign in the Pumpkin's mess hall that read THE MISSION: DEFENDING THE NORTHERN COMMUNITIES, and we believed this.

There was no ideology at all at the outpost, as far as I could see, no militarism and certainly no overt patriotism. For this generation Ben-Gurion and Herzl were streets. Were you inclined to speak seriously about such things you would be ridiculed, and no one was so inclined. The lives of the soldiers weren't governed by ideas. Neither was there any real hatred of the enemy, which seems so odd to me now that I asked a few of my friends if my memory was accurate. They agreed that although this might not be true of every unit in the army, it was true of ours. We were not averse to the idea of killing the enemy if we had to and would have been proud to have succeeded. But none of us remembered much animosity.

What kept things going on the hill was instead the usual dynamic in a small combat unit, as present in my unit as it had been in Avi's: the desire on the part of young men to be accepted and appreciated by their comrades and a fear of disappointing them. So successfully were these ties created in our platoon that they persist years later, when most of us have little in common. I would do any favor for any of them if asked at any time—not out of love, because we don't all love each other, but out of a residual loyalty that you would expect to go away but hasn't. We still meet at weddings, and for a barbecue every year on Independence Day. Shai, former sniper and current distributor of gourmet pasta; Dani the academic and Yoni the pension consultant; Ofir the shiatsu masseur; Adam the lawyer; Nadav the kindergarten teacher; Shachar, who does something for the Defense Ministry, no one knows exactly what. Ziv the carpenter doesn't make it much anymore, because it's hard to get around with eight sons.

Harel comes with his wife, Hila, a social worker, and their four boys. Wissam, one of our sergeants from basic training, who is still in the army and lives in a Druze town on Mount Carmel, usually shows up with his wife, Sabrin, an English teacher, and their kids Adham and Ward. (Wissam showed me one night in the desert that the stars of Orion's belt form the shaft of an arrow pointing north, and since then the great hunter and the Druze sergeant have been conflated in my mind.) Sometimes, after spending weeks together in the forced intimacy of the outpost during that first tour, we went home on leave, and only a day or two later arranged to meet of our own volition on the beach at Tel Aviv. No one understood us but us, so we needed to be together. In this country if you identify someone as a friend from the army, it is recognized as something different than saying friend. It's a different category.

# 35

THE PUMPKIN FINALLY introduced itself to me on the night
Natalie was going to get undressed. I remember the anticipation
with clarity because of the events of that evening but also because
of Natalie's unusual beauty—she was like an exquisite Sephardic elf,
bewitching even clothed.

The old TV set that struggled from one of the top bunks to pick
up the transmissions from Israel was advertising the upcoming episode of a dramatic series of no memorable merit. It starred Natalie,
an actress hardly older than us. In the advertisement, or at least in
the version replayed in my memory, you saw Natalie engaged in conversation before her right hand went toward her left hip and her left
hand toward her right, and she lifted the bottom of her shirt toward
her head, and there was nothing underneath—but at the crucial moment the camera cut away. The idea was that the viewer would have
to watch the episode to see the rest.

Amid our menial lives the importance of this moment of televised nudity can't be overstated, however pathetic it seems now. I believe that at this time most of us had yet to encounter the real thing.
After rotating out of the line and boarding a civilian bus home a girl

soldier would sometimes slip in next to me—a clerk or instructor coming from one of the safe bases inside Israel where such olive-drab unicorns roamed free, their uniforms concealing wild pinks and reds—and nothing more than the scent of synthetic flowers from her hair would render me senseless, sending my head falling forward, forcing my eyelids shut and the air from my lungs, my fingers clutching the grip of my rifle until my faculties returned. So potent was the effect of women's shampoo on my nervous system in those days that I am still vulnerable to it now.

When darkness arrived on the night of the television show the sergeants inspected the sandbags and machine guns around the perimeter, as they did each evening. I checked the battery on my night goggles, pressing my eyes against the rubber sockets and seeing the world in green. Things became more focused. We had been in the army for ten months and on the line for two. Less had happened so far than we had expected or might have hinted to friends at home. The hour of the TV broadcast was approaching when a lookout on another hill spotted three guerrillas moving up our ridge toward the Forest.

The message reached the Pumpkin on the radio. Harel summoned us, and I raced with him and seven others from the bunker to a vehicle that lurked like an enormous porcupine outside the gate, its back bristling with antennae and guns. There were two such vehicles on the hill, old Centurion tanks that the army had refitted to carry infantry in Lebanon, removing the turret and cannon and adding layers of armor to protect us from rockets and roadside bombs. I'm grateful for those efforts, which enabled the writing of this book.

One was equipped in front with a contraption of metal wheels that spun to detonate mines, and one was not. The choice was a matter of life and death, though this was not immediately clear. We took the latter, and the vehicle with the wheels was left behind. The driver slipped through his hatch, and when he turned the ignition the porcupine roared and belched a vile black cloud.

Four men were inside and the remaining four manned machine guns on the roof, legs in the vehicle, body exposed from the chest up: in front were Harel and our platoon sergeant, and in the rear I stood facing right, with my back to another soldier whose barrel pointed left. At my feet sat Yoni. Yoni was a medic, though this was purely a matter of accreditation, not experience, and he had never seen a wounded human being in his life. Yoni and I spent a lot of time during that tour singing some of the hits of the Backstreet Boys. I didn't know any of the good war poetry back then, in English or Hebrew, and wouldn't have appreciated it if I had. I was the radioman but wouldn't have known, for example, what to make of this radioman's prayer, part of which I translate here from the Hebrew:

*Lord of the Universe*

Please, increase your transmission strength
here I
can't hear, don't know
if once again you've stuck a metal flower in the antenna's
     lapel.
You're so gentle. Why
are you so soft, why are you always
civilian

Can you hear me clearly, over.
Roger, you too sound cut off, you
sound amputated, you

Are in a valley, deployed three-sixty. Hills
and a different Sea of Galilee. Please
apprise me of your transmission strength, with radar
we can't see your face, why
are you not on treads, why
are you not fighting, should we
send you a mechanized patrol, I
am full of faith
that it won't arrive and won't come back . . .

A new father and student of economics wrote that before he was called up by his reserve unit in the fall of 1973. He died along the Suez Canal; his name was Be'eri Hazak. And then there were the Backstreet Boys and "You are my fire / The one desire." Whether we knew it or not, as Israeli soldiers in the last years of the last century these were the poetic poles of our existence. It was the latter that Yoni and I had been singing. There was something comforting about it, and we weren't looking for insight.

Our vehicle rumbled southward on its treads down a low rise and then began working up a trail toward the unknown confines of the Forest, where we were to intercept the three guerrillas. By this time the Forest was assumed to be a lethal warren of trip wires and mines. Several stashes of Hezbollah explosives had been discovered there, and a plan to defoliate it with chemicals had even been considered.

We had never been inside. Our maps were practical affairs with eleva-
tion numbers, artillery targets, and code names, but here they might
have read *There be monsters.*

The vehicle strained to pull the weight of its armor up the hill,
and when we finally made it I caught a last glimpse of the Pumpkin
behind us. What had been the most dangerous place I could imagine
now represented all that was familiar and safe. Then we tilted down-
ward into the Forest with a shriek of springs and were alone.

I lifted my goggles and saw a green hand, mine, on the grip of
the green machine gun mounted in front of me, a shiny green band
of bullets running into the chamber from a box. Past the barrel was
impenetrable vegetation and—an invisible fist slammed into my face
and there was a red flash around the edges of the goggles and a low
thump that I felt in my stomach but don't remember hearing and a
hot breath of sulfur in my nostrils, perhaps not in that order, and I
dropped inside the vehicle and must have blacked out for a moment.

The next thing I remember is Harel speaking into the receiver:
*"Mit'an, mit'an."* Later we learned that a Hezbollah team had buried a
mortar shell under the trail and wired it to a large bomb buried a few
yards back and to a claymore concealed in the bushes. The shell blew
off our tread, the second bomb made a hole the size of a basketball
in the belly armor, and the claymore sprayed my corner with pellets.

Eventually the term *improvised explosive device* would enter everyday English, but that was still a few years away, and all I had was the
Hebrew military euphemism *mit'an*, which meant "payload." Proto-
types of growing efficiency were being perfected on us by masters of
the art. They calibrated the distance between the trigger, which was
the first mortar shell, and the other bombs based on a calculation of

the length of our vehicles with the mine-exploding wheels mounted on the front. We took the vehicle that didn't have that device and which was thus shorter by a yard. So instead of exploding directly under and beside the men in the center of the vehicle, in which case several of us would have been dead, the bomb and the claymore went off in the rear. The bomb penetrated the engine and not the cabin, and the claymore pellets pocked the side and flew harmlessly through the air by my head. A lighter vehicle would have been destroyed with many or all of its passengers.

I felt wetness on my face and thought it might be blood, but when Yoni checked, our faces so close our helmets touched, he saw nothing but soot and sweat. Harel called each of us softly by name. Everyone was alive.

I forced my head back out into the air. The explosives had crippled our vehicle and the engine, directly behind me, was on fire. This needed to be dealt with quickly because of the ammunition we carried in crates and strapped to our bodies, and I was closest. I climbed onto the roof, aware of my exposure to whoever was lurking in the undergrowth. I assumed they were there. My chest and stomach were tight. I hoisted out one of the twenty-liter water jugs and poured it into the engine, which steamed and hissed and stopped burning, and then scrambled back into the safety of the vehicle and pressed my index finger to the cool curve of the machine gun trigger. I remember being conscious of the wholeness of my body. I tried to get my breathing in order and waited for them to attack from the bushes. There were three of them out there.

They didn't attack. But the guerrillas had a mortar squad ready elsewhere in the vicinity, and soon came the whisper and the ground shook. We ducked inside, closed the hatches, and huddled together by the glowing green light of the radio as the shells drew closer. They seemed not to know exactly where we were and so were shelling along the length of the trail. They passed us, then hit the Pumpkin a few times before ceasing on schedule; they knew how much time they needed to get away before our batteries got their coordinates and started shooting back. The alien whirring of the first Israeli shell was audible as it arced over our heads into Lebanon a few minutes later, but by then our opponents were probably sipping tea in someone's living room with their weapons stashed under a bed. Around this time, on a flickering screen not three hundred yards away, Natalie peeled off her shirt in front of the rest of the Pumpkin garrison.

While we waited to be towed there were a few weak attempts at humor. "What doesn't kill you makes you stronger. What does makes your mother stronger"—standard jokes for the time. They weren't as funny as the joke underlying the whole enterprise, the punch line of which was delivered by trackers sent out the next morning to investigate. A Hezbollah team, they found, had set the explosives sometime in the recent past. But there were no guerrilla tracks at all from the night before, just the hoof prints of three wild boars.

# 36

THE MOST IMPORTANT event in both Lebanon and Israel that spring of 1998 was the World Cup in France. Soldiers huddled around the television with an intensity they rarely devoted to guard duty, and we saw Nabatieh draped with flags. The most popular was Brazil. The duty roster had to be carefully engineered because certain soldiers could not miss certain matches. It might have been our imagination, but the shelling seemed to drop off.

The showdown that everyone anticipated was between the national teams of America and Iran, our patron and theirs. If Iran lost, so went the joke, the men of Hezbollah were certain to take out their frustration on the representatives of American imperialism conveniently located on a hill overlooking their town. Being from one of the few corners of the earth where this sport is ignored, I knew nothing about it and could not help but notice that all the people here—the Israelis, the Lebanese—were joined by something that excluded me.

It was at around the same time that someone came up with the idea of executing a series of one-night ambushes on the hilltop directly to the south, on the outskirts of the Forest. The infantry had to venture out of the outpost on foot, or we were no better than the lookouts or cooks. In the "real war" our company was supposed to destroy enemy tanks using a venerable American rocket, the TOW, and because Hezbollah had no tanks the army had produced a version of this rocket that was supposed to work on people. The idea of the ambush was to use the launcher's thermal sight to spot guerrillas on the outskirts of Nabatieh and surprise them with a missile from an angle they were not expecting, and from far away. Far away sounded good to us.

We went through a few days of rehearsals. We removed candy wrappers so the crinkle wouldn't reveal us. One of the traditions in Lebanon at the time was to take a group photo before a mission while leaving space around the head of each soldier—this was to make things easier for the newspaper graphics people who would obtain the photograph and use red circles to indicate who had been killed. In our case this didn't represent true fatalism, though. We knew we were invincible. We loaded our weapons in unison and set out, the moon absent, the stars a brilliant smear across the middle of the sky.

Soon we were in low vegetation around the launcher's tripod. The cold got to work on me right away, though I was wearing an army sweater discovered at the bottom of a kit bag, which smelled as if it might have been used in 1967 to warm a dog. When it was my turn to look through the thermal sight I saw a version of Nabatieh appear in shades of red that corresponded not to gradations of light but to heat. It's a curious way to see a place. Some cars were colder than others, their engines having been inactive longer. Streetlights were hot. Boulders were cold. There were still people about, hot little shapes moving through cold streets, and I wondered if any knew there were soldiers looking down at them from the slopes above their town. I found the Cal-Tex gas station, al-Ghandour Hospital, a familiar minaret. Every so often I pulled myself away from the thermal sight and glanced around at my friends spread silently around the launcher, their backs to me, looking into the darkness with helpless human eyes that could see only light.

The tournament progressed, and the Iranians beat the Americans by the grace of God, 2–1. We enjoyed another quiet evening on our hilltop. On the very night that France was set to play Brazil in the finals, orders came down for another ambush. We spent the night outside, and out of pity the soldiers in the war room ran back and forth to the Pumpkin's TV set, checking the score and radioing updates to us.

Zidane—1–0 for France. This was passed around the squad in whispers. Then it was Zidane again, 2–0. Finally Nabatieh erupted. Cars began honking and driving up and down the streets with their headlights flashing. Music blared. From our position in the bushes we stared miserably down at their celebration. My radio murmured: France, 3–0.

A few nights later we were back. I had my eyes in the sight and saw the monastery of Saint Anthony and the abandoned villas. I scanned the dead zone between us and the town: a cow grazing, a few stray dogs. Another soldier, Ro'i, took my place, and I crawled away to guard the perimeter and wait for the night to be over. Harel mumbled acknowledgment of a radio transmission from the Pumpkin. Prepare to fire, he said.

We had done this so many times without seeing a thing that we no longer believed we ever would. We were slow to respond.

Move, he growled, and finally the soldiers in front of the launcher moved so they wouldn't be hit by the rocket as it flew forward, and the ones behind the launcher moved so they wouldn't be scorched by the blast. Harel was explaining something to Ro'i. The lookouts at the Pumpkin, who had better night vision equipment than we did, saw two guerrillas on the edge of the town. They were setting up what looked like a Sagger rocket outside someone's house. The lookouts were certain, and we could shoot when we were ready. Except for Ro'i with the thermal sight, none of us could see a thing. This drama was happening in the darkness a half mile away.

Are you on them? asked Harel.

It was a while before Ro'i said yes; the launcher's sight was primitive, and he wasn't sure at first.

Harel tapped his arm. Fire, he said.

A soft pop; a hiss lasting a long moment; then a roar as the yard-long rocket leapt from its tube. Ro'i began counting down seconds to impact, as we had been taught: Eight, seven, six. The red light of the engine swayed gently back and forth, growing smaller as the rocket hurtled away from our position on the ridge, passing out of the security zone and into Lebanon proper. In our little group crouching in the undergrowth there was silence except for the countdown—three, two, one, flash. I was surprised that an action we had taken on our side of the line had an immediate effect on the other side, as if the outpost and the town were part of the same world after all.

Ro'i saw hot shapes in the same spot, so we reloaded and he fired again. After the second rocket hit, a low boom came from a different part of the town: the guerrillas had a few other squads out that night. The lazy crimson glow of a Sagger passed in front of us from left to right, and we watched it explode on the embankments of the Pumpkin. Another one floated by and did the same.

Nimrod, a soldier with a vocabulary influenced by a childhood in the Dominican Republic—he called his rifle *pistola*, pronounced with an exaggerated Spanish accent and a dramatic twirling of the fingers—helped me dismantle the launcher. There was a thud and an odd buzzing sound, and for a moment something glowed a malevolent yellow on the ground between my boots and his. Later we understood it was shrapnel ricocheting off a rock, but just then it looked like black magic, and we stared at each other for an instant before diving behind some boulders and staying there until the shells stopped. The squad walked back to the outpost single file. By the time we arrived, thanks to overheard radio messages or rumors emanating from the war room, everyone seemed to have heard the story that we'd killed two enemy fighters. We were greeted like conquering heroes.

The lookouts in the surveillance post videotaped the incident, and they showed us the footage. It showed two guerrillas near a house, bent double and wearing backpacks, setting up their rocket. Then they disappeared. A few seconds later our first rocket hit a safe distance away. Our second was nowhere close. The guerrillas' ears might have been ringing, but both were alive and well. Maybe they still are today.

# 37

THE RAINY SEASON was over, the grass drying, the hills fading to light brown. Our time was almost up, and another company was set to replace us on the hill.

Just then the army decided to embark on some kind of commando excursion across the Red Line into Hezbollah territory, and our company was ordered to dispatch a squad from the Pumpkin north to Red Pepper. This outpost was manned by a crew from the South Lebanon Army, the Christian militia allied with Israel, and the raid was too secret for the militiamen. It was too secret even for us, the regular infantry, and we were told nothing beyond the fact of its existence. This happened with some frequency at the Pumpkin: soldiers with fancier gear than ours showed up, the garrison was kept in the dark, and after a while there was a buzz of activity as something extremely important happened and then the visitors disappeared, after which nothing changed and we were left doing the actual work of holding the line.

We took one of the armored porcupines and traveled to Red Pepper along the ridge road, arriving at a hill crowned with a squat concrete fort. A Russian tank of 1950s vintage sat by the gate; it was, like much of the militia's weaponry, Soviet-bloc materiel seized from Palestine Liberation Organization fighters in the 1982 invasion. I jumped down after Harel, radio on my back, and we walked into Red Pepper, just the two of us at first, like square kids stumbling into the wrong bar.

In a gloomy central room I found three or four men walking around in fatigue pants, some in T-shirts and others bare-chested, one with a fearsome scar on his torso. Soviet rocket launchers hung on walls of bare cement, next to nude pinups torn from a German magazine. One bearded man with a huge belly and tattooed arm was watching Hezbollah TV on a black-and-white set placed on a chair. On the screen two dignitaries in suits shook hands while other men in suits looked on. I eyed the tattooed man and the TV from a safe distance. The man turned to me, pointed to the screen, and said, "Duruz."

He meant that the men in suits were Druze. Perhaps he was Druze too. I wasn't sure, but he was, for reasons apparent only to him, trying to give this smooth-cheeked child a first lesson in the politics of his country. Or maybe he was just glad to have someone to talk to. I had been doing some reading and knew the name of the Druze leader in Lebanon, so I decided to try my luck. "Jumblatt?" I asked. I thought he seemed impressed.

"*La*," he said. No. He ignored me after that.

The South Lebanon Army was in many ways a familiar arrangement—the kind of local force you are theoretically supporting but which in fact supports you and follows your orders, more or less; which is usually said to be on its way toward operational independence but never quite arrives; and which in the end turns out to exist only as long as you are there. The militia was a remnant of the Lebanese civil war, when Christians in Lebanon's south allied themselves with Israel to protect themselves from Palestinian guerrillas and from their Muslim neighbors, but though the senior officers and some of the men were Christian, by the nineties many of the soldiers were Shiites and Druze who were in it for the salary Israel paid in American dollars.

Residents of the security zone—there were about two hundred thousand of them, mostly Shiites—had been severed from the rest of their country and were suspended between us and Hezbollah, sustaining themselves with agriculture, work permits for jobs inside Israel, and smuggling. Serving in the militia was one way to make a decent wage. Hezbollah also had money, of course, and its own agents and informers. In Khiam, a nearby town inside the zone, was a prison where officers from the militia and Israeli security agents worked the black arts on guerrilla suspects. We knew little of this, having no contact with anything beyond the immediate environs of our outpost. We had as clean a battlefield as one could hope for nowadays—anyone around the hill who wasn't us was an enemy, and we were to shoot them.

We were told that the Lebanese militiamen were our allies but that we were not to trust them because many had cousins in Hezbollah. They knew what we thought, and sometimes they had fun with us. One day a militiaman passing through the Pumpkin called over a friend of mine, leaned close, nodded toward Nabatieh, and passed on a tip in Hebrew. "Tomorrow they will fuck you," he said. They were fighting a different kind of war and played by different rules, and they scorned our moral pretensions. They spoke a different language.

A new Israeli commander at Beaufort Castle, a gentle kibbutz type, once entered Arnoun, the miserable village by the castle, after another attack on a convoy. He took a platoon of militia who began shooting and throwing grenades into the empty houses, their point being that the enemy had to think you were aggressive and a bit crazy. After that the new Israeli officer met the village headman and told one of his trackers, a Druze Arab, to convey to the headman in Arabic that the new Israeli commander was insane, *majnoun*, that everyone should be careful and not dream of letting the guerrillas anywhere near their homes. The commander was trying to speak the local language. The tracker turned to the headman and spoke for a long time, with expressive hand movements, and the officer asked what he was saying, because the original message was pretty simple. Everything's okay, said the tracker. When they arrived back at the castle the new commander got a call from his superior officer, a general, who had just been contacted by the United Nations. UN peacekeepers had a complaint from a village headman saying the Israelis were threatening to rape the villagers' daughters, burn their fields, and bulldoze their homes. Did the commander know anything about this? The commander called the tracker over and said, What the hell did you tell him?

What you told me to, replied the tracker, but in their language.

# 38

THE REST OF our squad clambered out of the porcupine and walked into Red Pepper, glancing cautiously around. The Lebanese militiamen vanished, leaving us in the new outpost under the bovine eyes of the naked Germans.

The toilet was a hole in the floor that had to be unplugged using a long metal stake, which brought ancient fecal matter bobbing upward with bubbles bearing a sulfurous reek from the bowels of the earth. We were attacked while asleep by savage mosquitoes. We ate canned corn and processed meat from combat rations. The view from the guard posts was unfamiliar and thus more sinister. We were at the northern end of the Ali Taher range and at the outermost boundary of the security zone; it felt as if we had traveled all the way upriver to the very end of everything.

Two special lookouts from the special unit doing the special operation that was the cause of our suffering used a special kind of camera to peer out at the towns inside Lebanon proper. As time went on we became increasingly homesick, not for Israel, which seemed like too much to ask, but for the Pumpkin. The company's time on the line was over, replacements were on the way, and everyone was supposed to rotate out within days. This was to be our salvation. But there were warnings of an attack on the road, and all convoys were canceled. No one could move anyway until the special operation, whatever it was, had taken place. A week went by, and then another.

Finally we were informed that the operation had been called off. Then someone else said this wasn't true and actually it had happened, but we hadn't noticed, and we weren't supposed to know because it was secret. It was all disinformation, apparently, but the army needn't have bothered, because we didn't care. We just wanted to go home.

# 39

WE ARRIVED BACK in a country no longer sure if the soldiers in Lebanon were heroes or victims. By this time you couldn't avoid the stickers saying GET OUT OF LEBANON IN PEACE. Support for an immediate pullout, recently a fringe opinion, was now common. The security zone had been crucial not long before, the lives expended there necessary. Now we started to hear that it might be a mistake. This was the thinking of many in the peace movement, which was to be expected, but there were even voices from the right who said so too. When a new government of the left was elected in 1999 it promised not only to try to make peace with the Palestinians and Syrians but also to pull the army out of Lebanon no matter what. This was supposed to happen within a year of the election, by the summer of 2000.

Now that it seemed a withdrawal was not only possible but imminent, the arguments became fiercer. Bruria's fax machine consumed and spit a constant stream of paper—letters, op-eds, hate mail, charts, plans for protests. Orna was outside the prime minister's official residence with another gimmick, a mock security zone outpost that the women had built. The mothers were getting so much attention that they looked like a mass movement. In fact, Bruria believes that at the biggest protest the Four Mothers ever held, one said by reporters to have included fifteen hundred people, there were not more than three hundred. She put the number of dependable activists in the dozens. It turned out not to matter, because if the photographers and TV cameramen liked you, they framed the image to show the people and not the empty spaces, so it seemed like more.

The mothers were driving across the country in convoys of bikes and jeeps, honking and waving signs, trying to convince people that soldiers were being sacrificed in Lebanon for no reason. But they often didn't say "soldiers"; they said "children." The idea that soldiers are children, everyone's children, the joint custody of all Israeli adults, caught on then and has never really gone away. This explains why a soldier's death here can be considered more tragic than the death of a civilian. The other guys, who were the same age, remained "terrorists."

It was around this time that Bruria's youngest son, Ofer, got out of the army and walked into an ambush.

Ofer thought his mother was right about the folly of the military's presence in Lebanon. He was vocal about it even during his service, which involved sleeping in bushes and trekking through riverbeds in pursuit of guerrillas, like everyone else. He had been an excellent soldier in one of the army's best reconnaissance outfits and was now a civilian again. At the height of his mother's campaign to get the army out of Lebanon, he sat down with a reporter and told him a story about something that happened northeast of the Pumpkin earlier that same year, 1999.

A detachment from Ofer's company set out from Outpost Basil

one night for a three-day ambush on a path used by guerrillas. When they reached the site, on the slopes of a hill called Qalat Jabur, two officers went ahead in the darkness to make sure the bushes were clear. The bushes were not clear, and the guerrillas waiting there opened fire and killed them both. A soldier charged in to help and was shot several times. His friends got him out breathing, but the guerrillas took his rifle; I mention this because I encountered the rifle later on.

Another officer, David, ran in and called for help, and Ofer heard. But he hesitated, or so he told the reporter.

"I didn't dare go down," he said. "I knew that whoever went would not come back. I knew that charging now meant dying in a stupid war." David died in the bushes. The headline of the interview with Ofer was "Why I Didn't Get Up."

Ofer didn't hide or run away. He fired his machine gun until it was hit by a bullet and put out of commission. At least some of the soldiers who were there don't remember him hesitating at all, they remember him fighting, and everyone knew the officer hadn't called Ofer by name. He called everyone, and no one went, and it might not have made a difference if they had. But in the interview Ofer seemed to be taking responsibility for everything. He was being honest about his politics because he was taught to be honest and because he thought the right thing to do was say it: This is a stupid war and dying in it is stupid. Had he kept quiet he would have been remembered by his friends as one of the unit's best soldiers and no one else would ever have known his name. Instead, in the popular imagination the entire mess at Qalat Jabur—and, by extension, the army's perceived failure of will in the security zone—became

Ofer's fault. He became known as the "machine gunner who didn't get up."

There were many in those years who believed that peace was coming, but there were also many who thought that peace was a dangerous fantasy that was eroding the country's will to fight. The kibbutz movement was part of the first camp, and the settlements were part of the second. Ofer was from a kibbutz, and worse, he was the son of a Four Mothers activist. The officer who called for help was from a settlement in the West Bank. Some on the right decided that one of their number had died a martyr, not just at the hands of Hezbollah but at the hands of the left. A rightist politician, a former general in the security zone, went on a lecture tour making that point, using Ofer as a symbol of rot among the general's ideological opponents, until one of the other soldiers present at the battle, who was from a settlement himself, happened to attend one of the lectures and was so incensed by the caricature of his friend that he wrote the politician a furious letter in which he only barely stopped short of calling him a liar.

The army's Education Corps turned the incident into a morality tale that became part of the curriculum for soldiers and officer trainees—a warning about letting your political beliefs interfere with your duty. In this version the vacillation of the machine gunner in Lebanon was contrasted with the bravery of another famous machine gunner, one from the battle of Ammunition Hill in Jerusalem in 1967. This gunner's name was Eitan, and there is a line about him in the popular song "Ammunition Hill": "Eitan didn't hesitate for a moment." Eitan ran ahead with his machine gun and died.

Someone from one of the settlements decided this still wasn't enough and appealed to the Supreme Court demanding that Ofer be tried for treason. Bruria and Ofer's father had to get their son a lawyer. After the court threw out the case Ofer went to India and stayed for years, and when he came back he went to live quietly on his kibbutz and today he won't talk about any of this at all.

# 40

THERE WAS, AND probably still is, a lovely restaurant on the banks of the Litani River near the Khardale Bridge in Lebanon—just a shack and a few tables set up along the water. The Pumpkin convoys went right past it. The existence of the restaurant never seemed reasonable, because we were in battle gear, with loaded guns, and believed ourselves to be in a war, and yet this restaurant was unwilling to acknowledge that. We gazed at it with puzzlement and longing every time we passed. We joked that one day when peace came we would sit there and watch the river run by.

The next time I took a convoy up to the Pumpkin I was a year older. Now I was a sergeant, second-in-command of a platoon, which meant that someone else carried the radio and I walked at the back of the line, keeping track of everyone, making sure they were drinking enough water, passing messages up to the officer in front.

I landed in the convoy yard next to two young soldiers who were looking around and waiting for an order. I grabbed one by the shoulder, aimed him toward the outpost, and said *Run*.

It was the spring of 1999, the beginning of the Pumpkin's last year. The army was trying to keep casualties down, and we saw the outpost had been fortified further: it was now covered entirely with a thick concrete ceiling, turning what had been the open courtyard into an indoor room. The space had been furnished with exercise equipment and an old couch hauled up on one of the convoys from the living room of someone's grandmother. We sent four of our soldiers to replace the guards from the outgoing garrison. I found a dirty kid seated on one of the bunks, holding his helmet like a bowl of soup he didn't feel like eating. He cursed when he saw me, but he wasn't angry, he was relieved, and he grabbed his rifle and pack and ran out toward the convoy and home. I was surprised to feel that I was home.

A day or two later I was patrolling the trench during Readiness with Dawn with a plastic cup of black coffee, dropping in on the sentries. The young ones were skittish and needed to be reassured. The sky was gray and the air cool, the hills around us quiet, the town below asleep. I rested my cup on a sandbag. Lebanon whispered something to me, but I was slow to react, and the shell exploded before I reached the floor of the trench. I felt the blast in my nose and caught a sour whiff of the powder. I ran in a crouch for the stairs leading down to safety.

Most of the soldiers had been dozing in their gear in the bunkers and were awake now, cursing the mothers and sisters of the Hezbollah gunners and their own officers and the army. "Launch, launch," said the loudspeakers, and a shell hit the new roof. It held. Assiag, one of the lieutenants, was demonstrating with a grin how he had run down from the trench without spilling any of his coffee. This was the nonchalance to which we all aspired. It helped to see this as a game won by the person who appeared least concerned.

# 41

Now that we were older and more experienced we laughed more, and our laughter was harsher. For the first time the argument among civilians about Lebanon was present in our conversations up on the line. Everyone knew about the Four Mothers by now. Most of us laughed at them—this wasn't a matter for mothers. But a few were willing to say they didn't understand what we were doing on the hill. Were we protecting civilians from infiltrations across the border? The guerrillas weren't attacking across the border anymore. When they wanted to strike Israel they simply fired rockets from deeper in Lebanon, outside the zone, and the rockets flew over the outposts and landed in Israel. Were we just protecting ourselves? And if that was the case maybe we shouldn't be there, and then we wouldn't have to protect ourselves? But if we left the border was exposed, and a whole new problem might be created, and it was hard to understand—you got to the point where you just wanted something to happen, anything, so you could blow off steam by shooting.

The sign that read THE MISSION: DEFENDING THE NORTHERN COMMUNITIES, which hung in every outpost in the security zone, was to remind the soldiers that in Lebanon were people who wanted to hurt our people and that we were here to stop them. It was a good idea to believe that, and it wasn't untrue—of course the northern communities did need defending. But the maze of our true situation was impossible to grasp then. It is hard to grasp even now.

Israel had gone into Lebanon all those years ago because of Palestinian guerrillas attacking across the border, but the Palestinian groups were long gone. The enemy had changed, and now it was Hezbollah. This group was Lebanese but created by Iran, the rising regional power, with the help of Syria, which controlled Lebanon. Hezbollah took orders from the dictatorship in Syria and from the clerics running Iran. Hezbollah was supposedly fighting to get us out of Lebanon, but Hezbollah leaders made clear later that they had rebuffed Israeli offers for a negotiated withdrawal. They didn't want us to leave; they wanted to push us out, which is not the same thing. By killing soldiers in the security zone they didn't convince Israelis to leave but rather that the security zone was necessary, and we dug in deeper and deeper to justify what we had already lost. This changed only with the helicopter crash, which had nothing to do with Hezbollah. Subsequent events show that they hoped to use their war against us to become the dominant power in Lebanon, which they went on to do with considerable skill. Their war seems to have always been as much for their country as it was against ours.

But even talk of goals like these is just a way that Western observers, with their disdain for religion and the power of the tribe and their unwillingness to take seriously the people involved in the conflicts they are observing, make sense of things to themselves. It's old-fashioned. In this new Middle East war was not just the means to an end, something terminated once a limited goal had been achieved.

Hezbollah's deputy secretary-general made this clear in a book he published in English, which is valuable reading. The idea, he wrote, was not to end the conflict on advantageous terms: Hezbollah is "not merely an armed group that wishes to liberate a piece of land, nor is it a circumstantial tool whose role will end when the pretext for using it comes to an end. It is a vision and an approach, not only a military reaction." When Hezbollah spoke of religious war against Israel and the West journalists interpreted it as rhetoric masking practical considerations. This, everyone was assured, would become obvious once the Israelis were out of Lebanon, which all could agree was a reasonable demand. But it turns out that Hezbollah and its many ideological cousins and imitators generally mean what they say.

What of the group's patrons in Syria? They wanted us not out of Lebanon but deep inside, because that way they could hit us through their pawns without risking their own army, which had been minding its own business on the Israel-Syria border since being bloodied there in 1973. That was why when Israel finally started talking about withdrawing from Lebanon, which would deny Syria the conveniences of the current arrangement, Syria's foreign minister declared that doing so without Syria's consent would be an act of war; it was a mental contortion memorable even by local standards. So by holding this hill and providing easy targets we served the interests of our enemies.

All of this makes you appreciate the simple genius of the copywriter who came up with "The Mission: Defending the Northern Communities."

By this time the army had ceased to be dismissive of the Four Mothers and was instead incensed. The commander of the Ali Taher sector, our part of the security zone, like most of his peers, thought the activists were meddling in affairs they didn't understand. (Much later this same officer became a teacher and a school principal, and today he uses the Four Mothers in class as an example of how civilians should behave in a democracy.) One general called them the "four rags" and had to apologize. The most famous of the Lebanon commanders, Gerstein, beloved of the troops and known for bravery, impolitic comment, and for stalking around the security zone bareheaded because he was too tough for a helmet, told a newspaper in that summer of 1999 that the protests were endangering the lives of our soldiers. If residents of south Lebanon thought we were leaving, he warned, they would switch their allegiance to Hezbollah. He also said the guerrillas were being weakened by our operations, that they had lost forty fighters since the beginning of the year. We were always winning and they were always being weakened, but somehow we never won and they never got any weaker, and a few months later they killed Gerstein with a roadside bomb.

# 42

ONE NIGHT A dozen of us laid an ambush not far from the militia position at Red Pepper. The army informed our friends from the South Lebanon Army that we were there, so they wouldn't shoot at us. It seems clear this is how Hezbollah found out. It's hard to blame the militiamen; by this time they understood that we were leaving and that they were on the wrong side. The air started to whisper soon after we arrived, and I lay down on the ground with my hands over my head. The first impact was a hundred yards away. We scattered, and I found myself crouching behind a boulder with a blond medic from a religious kibbutz in southern Israel.

There was another hiss. We both made ourselves as small as possible and stuck fingers in our ears, which I think was mainly something to do with our hands. A few yards away I saw three others behind a different boulder and heard the platoon's clown saying, We're going to die, we're going to die! But he was joking, and the other two were cracking up.

Hear, O Israel! cried the soldier, that being the prayer Jews say before death, and the other two laughed harder. There was another hiss and another impact. I knew there would be three or four more before the Hezbollah gunners stopped. The medic looked at me. He was pale, but he didn't say, I'm scared. He said, This isn't funny. As the sergeant I was one of the people in charge, and the implication was that I was responsible for this not being funny.

I told him everything would be fine, that it would be over in a second. This isn't funny, he said again, his tone rising. He was right. He had once treated two tank crewmen on a table in the mess, one in a coma and one without legs, so he knew this better than I. But admitting it wasn't funny was like the moment when a cartoon animal, having run off a cliff, renders itself vulnerable to gravity by realizing it is in midair. Laughter was our only cover out here. I was impatient with him.

One of our favorite jokes in those days was that we would come back to Lebanon one day as tourists. We would float down the Litani River on inner tubes and hike along the ridge. We would eat at the little restaurant on the riverbank, the one we passed on the convoys. We would return to the hilltop. We would sip coffee in Nabatieh. Maybe we would knock on the door of the Red Villa—maybe we would be invited inside and point to a hole in the roof and say, "I made that," and everyone would laugh. We would find the Babe.

We cast longing glances at the restaurant on the riverbank when we passed in our convoys and nudged each other and said, One day. Mainly these were just jokes about the absurdity of our lives. It's not that we actually expected this to happen, though in those years it didn't seem impossible. I believed peace was the default and conflict the anomaly, and so expected peace to arrive as a matter of course. In 1999 it still seemed the Middle East was changing for the better, and Lebanon still looked like the end of something bad, not the beginning of something worse.

# 43

Unlike Avi, I lacked the inclination or fortitude to write much. The only record I created while at the Pumpkin was a long letter, or maybe two, to a cellist in the Annex, the Toronto neighborhood where I was born. It must have seemed to her a barely decipherable interplanetary transmission. I would love to see these letters but have no idea where they, or the cellist, are now.

We went up and down the hill checking the side of the road for bombs, first the sniffer dog and its handler, then the tracker, then the platoon stretched out in the underbrush. We learned to recognize every rock in case a new one had appeared since our last sweep, the kind made of polyurethane and concealing a bomb. We eyed gum wrappers with suspicion as possible guerrilla traces. I tore my pants on thorns and sweated through my shirts and wiped my right hand on my webbing when it became too slick on the rifle grip. I set my feet down with care. Once, as we descended, I told a soldier in an armored personnel carrier to load the mounted machine gun, and he did, but it was already loaded. I was standing on the road in front of him. There were three or four bangs, the asphalt jumped, and little puffs of dust rose next to my feet. It was so close that we couldn't laugh about this right away but had to wait a few minutes.

Anyone with knowledge of other militaries would probably be surprised at how wholesome life was on the hill. Drinking, for example, was strictly forbidden, and if the rule was violated to any serious extent I never knew of it. I never encountered drugs, either, though years later I was informed of the ingenious double bottom of a Pringles can in the possession of one of the medics. There were no fistfights, few tattoos, and no pinups on the walls. The only picture I remember was of the curly hair and beatific visage of Meir Ariel, our poet, the prophet of an ordinary day at the beach, the "king anointed with salt, crowned in wreaths of seaweed"—this was before his music achieved the fame it deserved, and just after he died from the bite of a diseased tick.

There was a guitar, and a few books that were passed around. But the main form of relaxation during that tour involved a collection of videocassettes sent by one soldier's mother and played until they disintegrated. The most popular was *Starship Troopers*, about a war between futuristic soldiers and giant bugs. The men didn't seem to need much for life to be bearable inside the concrete bubble. But I spent little time in front of the television and instead found jobs to do up in the trench, watching the landscape, making sure the guns were greased and the ammunition crates full. The Pumpkin's new fortifications made our existence at the outpost easier, and I worried that they were making us soft. I didn't think the Hezbollah fighters were watching *Starship Troopers*, though now I wonder why I was so sure.

The soldiers seemed jumpier. There were more instances of guards opening fire at shapes in the night, and each time this happened I would awake to the thump of bullets from guns overhead and to the loudspeaker repeating, "Outpost attack," roll from my bunk, land on someone else, throw on my gear and run up to the trench to see tracers rebounding crazily off rocks around the hill. It was often the fault of a fox who skulked around the embankments and liked to startle the sentries. To the best of my knowledge the fox was never harmed.

Our company commander was Makov, a broad-shouldered officer with dark hair sprouting around the circumference of his collar, and a crooked gait that nearly kept him out of the infantry. Makov had arrived at the scene of the helicopter crash two years before and helped remove the bodies—but was careful, he said, not to look at the faces—and then went back to his sector in the security zone. A week or so after the crash he was hiding in a bush with an ambush squad when guerrillas discovered them and opened fire, and the guy next to Makov rolled onto him, bleeding, and others just slumped over, and what Makov did was charge out of the bush screaming *Forward* and shooting like a madman, and the guerrillas turned and ran.

I recently read Vasily Grossman's story about the pregnant Red Army commissar in Berdichev, and when he described the commissar's beloved—a gruff commander lost while charging with his men across a bridge—in my mind it was Makov. Like nearly all the officers to whom I answered as a soldier at the very bottom of Israel's infantry forces, he was competent and morally sound. His strengths were less in tactical finesse than in an instinctive understanding of the important things: he wanted to engage the enemy and destroy them, and he loved his men and wanted to protect them. After the tour he invited all of his officers and sergeants to his wedding, and it was a surprise to find that someone like that had parents and normal clothes.

Another memorable character around the outpost at this time was Amstel, a lithe and friendly sniffer dog—a German shepherd, maybe, or a similar breed. She was good company and good at her job. When we set out to check the access road for bombs she streaked ahead like a brown torpedo upon being released by her handler, then bounded back for a treat. She was around the outpost when off duty, and I became attached to her. She nuzzled me and wagged her tail, cheer and affection being qualities otherwise absent on the hill. A few months later, near another outpost, she triggered a bomb. Her handler was wounded and Amstel disappeared, never to be seen again. Perhaps she was spooked and ran away into the brush, changing from a trained Israeli army dog into a Lebanese stray. Or, as seems more likely, she had simply been blown to pieces, which is what she was for.

# 44

Now Blutreich is the best rock climber in Israel, but then he was just a young lieutenant with his soldiers, the Pumpkin's greenest platoon. It was the spring of 2000 and it was almost over, that was clear. Almost but not quite. My own time in the army had just ended, so for me it was over anyway. I believe that by this time, like many Israelis, I had replaced one simple idea—"The Mission: Protecting the Northern Communities"—with another, that ceding the security zone to our enemies would placate them. The government's deadline for a withdrawal was close, and few seemed to believe in the zone anymore. But the outposts were still there. It was that arbitrary window at the end of a war, a time we might name for Pvt. Henry Gunther, twenty-three, of Baltimore, Maryland, killed after the final German surrender of 1918 but one minute before the armistice technically came into effect.

The entire position was now covered in a new kind of black camouflage net that was supposed to make movement behind it invisible. The soldiers almost never went outside anymore, because the army was worried about losing men so close to the end. The guard posts were empty. Instead soldiers sat in the trench looking at screens attached to cameras that they moved with joysticks. The cameras had been installed after the guerrillas turned out to be adept at hitting guard posts with antitank missiles. That January they killed a soldier at one base, and a week later they killed three more somewhere else. Not long after he arrived at the Pumpkin, Blutreich went inside one of the posts and found it still charred. When he bent down to look at a dark patch on the floor he saw it was a piece of someone's scalp.

Journalists had begun reporting that soldiers were scared to serve in the security zone. "No one wants to be the last person killed in Lebanon," one reporter wrote, in what became one of the themes of those months. This was true. At Beaufort Castle was a kid named Tzahi who didn't want to be the last person killed in Lebanon either, but he was.

"The soldiers entering Lebanon project a sense of dejection," read a subheadline in the daily *Yediot Ahronot*. "They feel that they're going to die, and they don't know why." The words accompanied a photograph of a helmeted soldier looking at the camera from behind sandbags. As it happened, the soldier was me. A news photographer had arrived once during an earlier tour, and an editor must have pulled it from a file.

According to the accepted story, the fear and uncertainty of the final months in Lebanon caused the soldiers to fall apart. A movie made about this time, *Beaufort*, gives that impression. This works as a dramatic flourish and makes it feel like the Vietnam movies we've all seen: soldiers battling their own demons and each other, struggling to remain sane while pursued by a faceless enemy in a conflict shorn of politics and context. It makes for a better plot, and were this a work

of fiction I would be tempted. But it didn't happen that way. Whatever the soldiers hanging around the border liked to tell reporters,
the soldiers I knew, the ones in the dangerous bases inside Lebanon,
didn't fall apart. The companies on the line functioned until the very
end. I feel both entitled and obligated to say this as the soldier who
served for a moment as the poster boy for our demoralization.

Being imprisoned behind the fortifications didn't make the soldiers feel safer. It's easier to imagine things when you're passive. One
of the militia posts nearby was hit one day by something big, no
one knew what it was, and the soldiers at the Pumpkin were told
that Hezbollah now had a weapon that could penetrate the concrete
roof. The soldiers thought it might be some kind of drone, but the
army wasn't telling them anything, only that the next target was the
Pumpkin. In retrospect we know it was a substantial rocket manufactured in Iran, which was bad enough, but the secrecy made it seem
even worse, a "Judgment Day weapon," as one of them remembered
later on. There was a rumor that rescue teams with cranes and jack-
hammers were standing by in Israel to come and dig the garrison's
remnants from the ruins.

On the day it was supposed to happen the last Pumpkin commander was up in the trench during Readiness with Dawn, waiting. He was a wry twenty-eight-year-old named Kahana. A few shells
whizzed into the embankments and wounded one of the surveillance
guys, but that wasn't it yet. It wasn't big enough. Kahana crouched,
folding his long limbs into the trench, and something hissed in from
the west. This time he felt the concussion in the pit of his stomach
and the whole hill shuddered. When he peeked out he saw a dust
cloud rising just to the north. The thing had missed. A few Israeli

jets were in the air waiting to destroy the launcher once it fired, and they swooped down, and the soldiers never heard more about it. If nothing else, the incident shows that if you're facing men dug in and immobile on hostile ground, you don't need to do much but leave them to their imaginations.

# 45

TRUCKS ARRIVED CARRYING hundreds of olive discs, twenty-five-kilogram mines, which would blow up the Pumpkin when the pullout order was given. There were so many that the garrison had nowhere to put them all, so they stacked them under beds and inside unused ovens. The pair of army engineers who appeared with the explosives told the soldiers not to worry, because the mines weren't live until they inserted detonators. But that wasn't as reassuring as the engineers seemed to think, and no one was sure that if the Hezbollah gunners scored a direct hit now the whole place wouldn't explode.

The soldiers packed all unnecessary gear and sent it down to Israel. The telephone line was cut. Most of the soldiers were sent down themselves, and by the end it was just Kahana, the commander, and Blutreich and his new platoon, not even a year in the army, and a few tank crewmen—maybe two dozen in all. When they walked around the trench at night the very dimensions of the outpost seemed to have changed. The distance between the guard posts felt longer. The hill became darker, more desolate, as the landscape closed in and the outpost slipped from Israeli hands.

Things were pretty ragged by the end. One day a few South

Lebanon Army militiamen on their way past the Pumpkin in an armored vehicle were hit by a mine or a rocket, and one of their officers stumbled up to the Pumpkin's gate without one of his hands. The engineers began distributing the mines around the outpost, but there were still no detonators, they said, so there was no reason for concern.

The end came ahead of schedule, on a Sunday in late May. A civilian parade organized by Hezbollah crossed from Lebanon proper into the security zone and approached a South Lebanon Army outpost. The Lebanese militiamen fled, and their commander cannily joined the marchers. There were more processions toward militia outposts the next day. When our aircraft fired at the road in front of the marchers to hold them back they just walked off the asphalt and continued in the brush, daring the pilots to shoot them. The pilots didn't shoot. After that the militiamen near the Pumpkin abandoned Red Pepper, Cypress, and Citrus. And just like that, the security zone disintegrated.

That evening the order was given to arm the mines and prepare to abandon the Pumpkin at 11 p.m. There was no one friendly anymore for miles around, and if the soldiers waited too long they might have to fight their way home. The engineers went around priming the mines, but then a different order arrived, everything was postponed again, and the soldiers prepared for one more day.

The guerrillas knew it was the end and wanted the Israelis to leave under fire. I suppose they figured there was no point in conserving their ammunition if there wouldn't be anyone to shoot at tomorrow. The barrage started early the next morning and hardly let up after that. At nightfall Kahana, the company commander, said again: We're leaving at eleven. Before the appointed time Kahana pulled the sentries from the guard posts. It was quite possibly the first time the Pumpkin had been unguarded in nearly the entire lifetime of some of the soldiers who were there that last day.

The men ran down to the tanks and armored porcupines. Inside the outpost they left a metal tray of uneaten chicken schnitzels, which were destined to remain forever under the rubble. Perhaps an archaeologist would find the tray someday and ponder it as a relic from the conflicts of antiquity, a modest sacrifice to the war gods.

The little procession of vehicles waited two hundred yards from the outpost, not even close to the distance the safety manuals mandated from an explosion the size of the one coming. The engineers ran a white fuse down from the hilltop to a small hand trigger with two plastic handles, like one of those devices squeezed to relieve stress. Kahana had the trigger. Just then the barrage lifted, for some reason, and things were quiet.

There was a flash to the northeast and then a boom—Outpost Basil was gone. It was eleven o'clock.

Something flared a few miles to the south and Blutreich, the lieutenant, saw the outpost at Beaufort Castle blow up—white, red, and orange, explosion after explosion, the sky illuminated as if the sun were rising behind the crusader fort an hour before midnight. That's when Hezbollah opened up again, heavier than before, but it wasn't too bad because they were hitting the Pumpkin, which was empty now. There were jets roaring around, bombing guerrilla positions in the hills to the north, helicopters overhead, drones too, as if the whole air force had come out for this final act. The two dozen men clustered on the hill felt small.

Nearly all the outposts were gone, the last soldiers on the roads moving south toward Israel. Every officer in the army seemed to be yelling on the radio. Someone was saying one of the tanks leaving Beaufort was hit. A drone operator saw it burning. Authoritative voices shouted instructions and ordered other authoritative voices to shut up and clear the frequency. It was like the apocalypse, Blutreich remembers, the night sky alive with aircraft and the hills of south Lebanon emitting fire as if they had been volcanoes all along, merely dormant for all of the years of our presence.

The young officer looked over at the company commander and saw him grip the trigger. Blutreich ducked and plugged his ears. The commander's fist clenched, pressing the handles together. Nothing happened.

Kahana pumped the trigger again, and then a few more times.

He took two soldiers and sprinted back up toward the empty outpost, running the fuse through his hand and finding it intact. When he reached the entrance a tank on another hill spotted figures moving around the Pumpkin and thought they were guerrillas, because it was after 11 p.m. and the soldiers were supposed to be gone. The tank commander said on the radio that he was about to fire, and Kahana heard it all but couldn't break through—the radio was so busy you couldn't get a word in, so no one heard him screaming, It's us, it's us. It was a bad moment, but someone else got to the tank just in time.

Kahana left the outpost again, dispirited, and rejoined his band of soldiers downhill. He had run out of ideas. He would be the only commander who failed to carry out the order to destroy his outpost. The Pumpkin would be the only base left standing.

He had the trigger in his fist and was still pumping, but he had given up, which was why his back was turned when the charge finally took.

Blutreich was standing in one of the vehicles looking up at the concrete structure atop the hill, and he thought he was dead, that's how bright the flash was, like a thousand cameras going off at once. For years he couldn't be photographed. He thought at first that he'd been hit by a missile. By the time he determined that he was alive the sky was raining ash and chips of concrete.

# Part Four

# 46

AROUND THE TIME the last soldiers crossed back into Israel before dawn on May 24, 2000, I unlocked my bike outside my parents' house in their town near the Lebanon border. I rode along the Mediterranean in the weak light and then turned inland through an Arab village where only the roosters were awake, and then through sunflower fields and avocado orchards to the greenhouse where I had a job growing roses for export.

By then I had been a civilian for a few months. The military's absence from my life still felt like the first disconcerting steps off a moving airport sidewalk, the withdrawal of an unseen force propelling me forward. I became accustomed only gradually to being unarmed and responsible solely for myself. University would begin in the fall, and there would be travel, a job, a family, the same ideas we all had, more or less, though none of us thought everything was going to happen so fast. When we get together now we look at each other and at our wives and children, and it hardly seems possible. In the years that elapsed since that morning and the recording of these experiences, between our early twenties and mid-thirties, our sense of what fate might hold for us opened so wide it seemed to encompass the whole world and then began to narrow again, which turns out to be the way it works.

Each morning at the greenhouse I found my shears and apron and got to work cutting the roses that were about to bloom in red, yellow, white, and pink. The flowers were always budding, spreading leaves and petals. Every morning there were thousands more.

The sun wasn't up and no one was quite awake. It was a good way to start a day, breathing humid, perfumed air, listening to the murmuring of the volunteers from Germany and Holland, a few Arab kids, some Ethiopian immigrants from an Absorption Ministry trailer camp down the road. There was a mild man from one of the Israeli Druze towns in western Galilee, a sculptor in his spare time, who had spent part of his army service in Lebanon with the infantry. We understood each other. We worked for a while in parallel rows. He nodded through the glass panes toward the border with Lebanon.

They just pulled out, he said. I stopped clipping.

In the daze after my discharge I hadn't been following things closely. It was behind me, and what was before me seemed more interesting.

They left Lebanon, he said, that's it. He heard it on the radio driving over.

At that moment the border crossings in the Finger of Galilee were clogged with armored vehicles coming south out of the security zone, and there were long lines of Lebanese militiamen and their families trying to escape to Israel. Every news crew in the country was there filming the soldiers coming out grinning and waving flags. Bruria and Orna were also present—they heard the news in the middle of the night, drove up to the border together, and were watching it all happen in disbelief. I knew my old company was in there somewhere but didn't have a way to reach anyone. All I knew was what the other worker had said: that the security zone, that whole world that had existed the evening before, was gone, and with it the Pumpkin.

I don't think we said more. It made sense to me at that moment. Things were changing in my life and in the life of the country, old things were being destroyed and new things were coming that were better. The fulcrum of Israel's recent history can be found in those months in the spring, summer, and early fall of that year.

Had you told me then that I would still be thinking about the hill years later, that I would try to return to it in person and then again in writing, I would have been surprised. I was twenty-two and wasn't sure anything was indelible. So I got back to work, holding the stem of each flower with the gloved fingers of my left hand and snipping it with my right, and the sky outside the glass grew light as always. There was a new century ahead of us.

# 47

AFTER I ARRIVED at the university campus in Jerusalem not long afterward, enrolled in the department of Islamic and Middle Eastern studies, students with familiar faces sometimes approached me in the halls. It would be someone from a tank crew, or one of the lookouts, now with longer hair and jeans. You're from the Pumpkin, one of us would say, and we'd shake hands and grin but wouldn't have that much else to add. We shared something we knew was significant, being from the Pumpkin. But even then, not six months after the pullout, it was becoming clear that the significance was apparent only to us.

The sites of Israel's famous battles have tended to remain afterward within our borders: Ammunition Hill, the Kastel hill above the Tel Aviv–Jerusalem road, Tel Faher in the foothills of the Golan. There are signs and guided tours. Survivors can visit with their children and stand there in safety. But when the Pumpkin was abandoned with its sister outposts in the spring of 2000 it became inaccessible, controlled by our enemies on the other side of a hostile frontier. Lebanon might have been the moon. Our society hardly paid a thought to the security zone war once it ended. Israelis were soon preoccupied with other events. They were also afraid that if they looked too closely they might reach, and then speak out loud, the conclusion that it had all been an error. And it is easier to forget drawn-out affairs like ours than brief incidents of high drama, like a war lasting six days, just as a heart attack would stand out in the memory more than a decade of chronic pain, though the chronic pain might be more important in shaping who you are.

And of course everyone would rather remember victories. Whatever this was, it wasn't that. "Except for the bereaved families and the fighters who served here, who carry in their heart experiences they can share with no one, this war will be forgotten in a few years," wrote the most insightful commander of the Lebanon era, Chico Tamir, after the withdrawal. "The discomfort the army felt about the results of the war, I thought, and the deep wounds it left in Israeli society, sped up the rapid repression of memory that was already under way." Army operations less significant or costly than the years of the security zone have been given official names and military ribbons, but this period was granted neither. The only memorial to the Lebanon dead is an unauthorized one, built by Orna on her kibbutz with no help from the government.

Only a fraction of Israeli men serve in combat units, and not all combat units were engaged in Lebanon. The traditional pipeline of information from the military to Israel's populace is the reserve army, civilians called up for short periods of service in units that tend to be democratic and unruly. Reservists often feel moved to complain, write a letter to someone in parliament, or publish something. But in the nineties the army didn't use reservists in Lebanon, perhaps for this reason, and kept the zone mostly off-limits to reporters. The fighting was thus left to the unformed minds of regular soldiers just out of high school who barely understood what they were seeing.

Back in civilian life the soldiers of the security zone saw no reflection of our experience, no indication that anything important had happened. One of our characteristics was a kind of feigned indifference, a ban on admitting that anything that happened to us mattered, and this pose turned out to be hard to discard even afterward. It added to the general forgetfulness. So did the fact that most soldiers, even at the most dangerous outposts, never experienced anything worthy of calling a "battle," let alone a "war," so it hardly seemed right to claim any accomplishment amid the greater feats of our fathers and grandfathers. After a while even the physical existence of a place like the Pumpkin started to seem unlikely. It was just one of those inexplicable things that happen to you when you're young. Or maybe none of it had happened at all.

# 48

WHEN THE SUICIDE bombings began in our cities that fall we realized there was no "new Middle East" after all. That phrase would never be used again without sarcasm. The Middle East was gutted buses and cafes, and young killers in black masks.

It turned out the Palestinians were watching closely that last night in the security zone, earlier the same year. That night was "a light at the end of the Palestinian tunnel, a hope that liberation might be achieved by treading the path of resistance and martyrdom," wrote Hezbollah's deputy secretary-general. "What happened in Lebanon can be repeated in Palestine." Israelis had elected a government that would end the military occupation of the West Bank and Gaza and make peace, but now the peace talks collapsed. For the Palestinians there would be no more humiliation or compromise, just as Hezbollah had brooked none. Watching Palestinian television, I saw yellow Hezbollah flags appear at rallies. Propaganda videos showed riots in Gaza with clips of Israeli vehicles leaving the security zone.

The humanities faculty of Hebrew University is in a concrete fort of a campus set atop Mount Scopus. In the university's walls in those days I studied Islam as an idea that touched a nerve in Arabia long ago and showered countries with spires and domes, poetry and prophecy in flowing letters, empires coming together like drops of mercury and splitting apart like amoebas. I spent an hour in my course "The Modern Middle East," which appeared in our textbooks to be a safe distance away, and then packed my books and exited into the modern Middle East, where a woman named Andalib, who was a few years younger than me, could walk into the open-air market in Jerusalem a few minutes after I walked out, press a button sending an electric charge to her explosives, and kill herself and six people who happened to be standing nearby. A youth with a knapsack sometimes had the effect on me of that old whisper in the sky over the Pumpkin. Sometimes you heard a deep thump, then silence, then sirens, and everyone knew what it meant.

After our withdrawal the south of Lebanon came under the control not of the Lebanese government but of Hezbollah. Guerrillas crossed the border into Israel that fall, unhindered by any security zone, killed three soldiers and took their bodies. Later, two guerrillas infiltrated into western Galilee and waited along a road. When a truck arrived they killed the driver, and then a woman in her car, then a mother and her daughter who happened by after that. They saw a farmer tending his sheep nearby and killed him; he was my future wife's cousin. In a different incident guerrillas shot two army technicians off a frontier antenna. Nearly everyone agreed that pulling the soldiers out of the outposts in Lebanon was the right decision. It was, because this gave our enemies fewer targets and made it harder for them to attack. But our move turned out to have no bearing on their intentions. Their war against us was still on after all.

I answered a reserve call-up in 2001 and spent a few weeks

patrolling near the Lebanon border. I saw Hezbollah men in the open for the first time, manning guard towers by the fence. We weren't allowed to shoot them, and they seemed to be under similar orders. Once, on a patrol, one of their guards smiled at us as our jeep passed and used his hands to mime an explosion. I took this to mean he hoped we blew up, which was fair enough, but then our cell phones began to ring. A suicide bomber had just detonated himself in a pizza restaurant in Jerusalem, erasing a few families. The Hezbollah man knew before we did.

For a while the word *Lebanon* started showing up in newspapers again. When Palestinian gunmen ambushed a bus in the West Bank, crippling the vehicle with a bomb and machine-gunning the passengers as they fled, the headline the next day was "Just Like Lebanon." Soldiers in Gaza and the West Bank began to move in convoys, and roads were swept for bombs. Hezbollah men and their Iranian patrons appeared among the Palestinians with money, weapons, and advice, and the Palestinians increasingly expressed their opposition to us in the language of holy war.

The military reserve called me up again in the spring of 2002, at the peak of the violence, and I left the university and found myself back in a hilltop outpost with my friends. This time we overlooked the West Bank city of Nablus, which the army had placed under siege. Passover was coming, and the unit's cooks spent days preparing food for the seder. Mixed with the usual army smells of gun grease and sweat were those of spicy Moroccan fish and chicken soup. But the meal never took place. As we sat down to eat at long tables in the mess someone started shooting at the outpost. We all scrambled up into the trench and shot back, not that we could see the assailant, who was in one of the nearby homes. While this was going on news passed along the line of men. A suicide bomber had struck a seder at a hotel in the city of Netanya. There were thirty dead.

Within days the army had called up thousands of men, and mobile command posts appeared at the outpost. I saw a line of infantry descend at night toward the buildings of Nablus, where they moved from house to house by blowing holes through the walls and fought in neighborhoods defended by armed guerrillas and full of innocent and terrified people, many of whom were killed beside their fighters. That week a squad from our brigade, temporary soldiers like us, walked into an ambush in the city of Jenin and thirteen of them died.

I stood in the middle of the night at one of the checkpoints ringing Nablus when a bus pulled up. Out came a few dozen Palestinian men, who began crossing through the island of harsh light into the darkness of their city. "Rejects," an officer said, dismissing them with his hand. He meant they were detainees from one of the army's sweeps, seized, cuffed, questioned, and released after being deemed worthless to our intelligence people. I saw one man my father's age, with a graying mustache and unshaven cheeks, shuffle by a few paces away in leather dress shoes but without socks. He didn't look at me.

From a third-floor office in downtown Jerusalem I heard a suicide bomber detonate himself one rainy morning and saw a trail of white smoke curl upward from the scene. A bomber struck a line outside a club in Tel Aviv popular with Russian kids—Maria, Ylena, Irena, Sergei, Alexei, twenty-one dead in all. Eventually the modern Middle East penetrated the university itself and killed nine people with a bomb in one of the cafeterias. I wasn't on campus when it happened, but my sister was—she was in a different cafeteria and saw them bring the bodies by. You might remember Jonah, my child-hood friend, who recited Poe to himself one night in his tank at the Pumpkin. His younger brother Daniel, a playmate of mine from To-ronto backyards, who by this time was a junior officer in the Fighting Pioneer Youth, a pianist and student of the Irish pipes, was leading a squad trying to arrest or kill a gunman in Nablus when he was shot in the side. The round slipped between the plates of his bulletproof vest and there was nothing anyone could do.

The Israel that believed in compromise, a country rooted in the old left of the kibbutz movement, was shattered. The left went from ascendant to defunct in a matter of months. The triumph of the Four Mothers was, in retrospect, the last charge of the kibbutzniks, the final instance in which those Israelis would lead anything of national importance. By the end of the pivotal year, 2000, they receded into the margins, where they remain.

Amid these events came the suicide attacks at the World Trade Center and the Pentagon, and the Americans were soon in Afghani-stan and then in Iraq. Then came the same roadside bombs, the same videotaped explosions shown on TV again and again with a sound track of martial music, televised farewells from martyrs, clerics lead-ing militias with black uniforms and headbands, the idea that war is not a means but a way of life and that death is victory—all the ele-ments of the Hezbollah technique, perfected against us in the years of the Pumpkin, broadcast via satellite TV to the Arab world and beyond throughout the nineties, crowned by the victory of 2000, and applied by the children of the nineties against the new invad-ers. Sometimes it wasn't just the same tactics but the very same peo-ple. Hezbollah, one American intelligence man said after a few of

the group's operatives were picked up in Iraq, was the "A-team"—
al-Qaeda was just the "B-team."

Of course the Americans did what we did, which was armor their
convoys and become heavier and slower the more men they lost, and
dig in and build hilltop outposts to control hostile territory, all of
them very important until they were not and were abandoned. It felt
as if by squeezing the trigger on that last night in the spring of 2000,
my friends had freed a wrathful millennial spirit trapped inside the
hill and released it into the world.

# 49

I was sitting not long ago along one of the boulevards in Tel Aviv. The Middle East had succumbed to chaos and butchery dwarfing our own conflict in one tiny corner of the region. But our country was calm again, at least for a time, thanks not to anyone's goodwill but to the force of our arms.

The promenade was full of teenagers in tank tops, tattooed riders of old-fashioned bikes, men with women and men with men and women with women, speaking the language of the Bible and of Jewish prayer. There were old people sipping coffee outside a restaurant, and some music. The country was going about its improbably cheerful business on a weekday evening.

Beyond the city were the neighborhoods of middle-class apartments with parking lots of company Mazdas, the kinds of places where I found many of the men from the Pumpkin when I went looking for them to write this book, most having first passed through Goa or the Andes for decompression before coming back to their families, finding work as programmers and accountants and settling down to watch their kids on the swings. All of this is more than our grandparents, the perpetual outsiders of the ghettoes of Minsk and Fez, had any right to expect. But it seemed for a moment—and this can happen to me in a cafe in my corner of Jerusalem, or picking up my children at school, anytime—that the buildings on either side of the boulevard were embankments, and the sky a concrete roof.

The Israel that arrived in Lebanon in 1982 was still imaginative and light on its feet, however unwise its ideas and however wretched their execution. The point is that we thought we could make things happen. The invasion was supposed to effect a dramatic change in our surroundings, just as in the nineties, the years of this narrative, many of us believed that such a change would be engineered not by force but by compromise. Underlying these very different enterprises was the same sentiment—our fate was malleable, and it was ours to shape. But most of us came to understand in the year of the Pumpkin's destruction that we were wrong. We might make good choices, or bad choices, but the results are unpredictable and the possibilities limited. The Middle East doesn't bend to our dictates or our hopes. It won't change for us.

When these things began to be clear something interesting occurred. People in Israel didn't despair, as our enemies hoped. Instead they stopped paying attention. What would we gain from looking to our neighbors? Only heartbreak, and a slow descent after them into the pit. No, we would turn our back on them and look elsewhere, to the film festivals of Berlin and Copenhagen or the tech parks of California. Our happiness would no longer depend on the moods of people who wish us ill, and their happiness wouldn't concern us more than ours concerns them. Something important in the mind of the country—an old utopian optimism—was laid to rest. At the same time we were liberated, most of us, from the curse of existing as characters in a mythic drama, from the hallucination that our lives are enactments of the great moral problems of humanity, that people in Israel are anything other than people, hauling their biology from home to work and trying to eke out the usual human pleasures in an unfortunate region and an abnormal history.

It seems to me now that the Lebanon outposts were incubators for the Israelis of the age that followed the outposts' destruction: allergic to ideology, thinkers of small practical thoughts, livers of life between bombardments, expert in extracting the enjoyment possible from a constricted and endangered existence. The former soldiers are people used to political currents of immense complexity and capable of ignoring them. They didn't come back from Lebanon and devote themselves to politics, defense, or settling the frontiers but rather to the vigorous and stubborn building of private lives, and these combined energies have become the fuel driving the country. Israel isn't a place of slogans anymore, certainly not the Zionist classics "If you will it, it is no dream," or "We have come to the Land to build and be rebuilt." But if one were needed now, why not recall Harel's laconic explanation of how he went back to the army after the funerals of every single member of his platoon but him? I don't think we could do better than "On the bus."

When Hezbollah attacked a border patrol inside Israel in the summer of 2006, triggering a month of fighting, my parents' town was hit by several hundred rockets and was nearly deserted. I reported the war and remember the sinister sight of traffic lights blinking yellow along a main street devoid of pedestrians or traffic. The day after the shooting stopped the town filled with people as if nothing had

happened. Less than a year later I counted eight new cafes and res-
taurants on the same street.

Making do in this way is perhaps a fundamental national ability, something Jews have done throughout the centuries no matter
how inhospitable the soil. It reminds me of the impromptu rave that
erupted in one of our bunkers one night in 1999, with shirts off,
military light sticks glowing green and orange, and "The Rockafeller
Skank" on repeat. Laughter inside the perimeter; outside, the quiet
of the trench and young men in guard posts.

This is all, in other words, very familiar. Sometimes the Pumpkin
seems more present to me now than it did when it existed.

# 50

A CANADIAN FRIEND of mine arrived in Israel one day after backpacking through Lebanon. She was unmindful of our borders and couldn't understand why I was struck by the ease of her transit. If you were Israeli the border was like a high steel wall, and beyond it were people who wanted you dead. But if you were Canadian the border hardly existed, and Lebanon was just a place. This hadn't truly occurred to me until then.

The plan had its roots in the jokes we used to tell as soldiers about coming back to the security zone one day as tourists. But now it began to take shape in earnest in my mind. The Middle East was closing in on me. But what if I ignored the borders it wanted to impose and went to Lebanon again, protected not by armor or sandbags but by the accident of my birth in a country far away? I would see the hill without fear and privately mark the end of that time. I would meet the people I had glimpsed through binoculars and tread their sidewalks with them. I would share something of their lives. I'm sure that at the time I thought this might give me reason for hope.

I understood that I would be detained upon landing at the airport if my identity became apparent. I knew too that I would have to cross into territory controlled by Hezbollah. It was a little more than two years since the withdrawal. The guerrillas were holding a live Israeli hostage, a crooked businessman they had abducted some time before in the Persian Gulf, and three Israeli soldiers whose fate was unknown. But I had a clean Canadian passport. I had what I thought of as my Canadian face, a look of benign vacancy that seemed to induce in Middle Easterners not suspicion but a desire to give me directions without being asked. I was twenty-five. I could pull it off.

I flew to Toronto and spent a few weeks there, becoming accustomed to drooling my vowels again instead of spitting them. I cut the Hebrew labels out of my clothes. I flew to London, changed airlines, and left all incriminating documents and spare Israeli change at the apartment of a friend. The story would be that I was from Canada, a university student of Islam and the Middle East. This was true, strictly speaking, though it left much out.

# 51

AN HOUR BEFORE dawn: the red blink of wing lights through the mist outside, stale air, the drone of engines—a routine flight from Heathrow. When the stewardess looked at my stub as I boarded a few hours before I thought she might laugh and send me back. But she said 23C was right this way, sir, and enjoy the flight, and before she finished speaking her smile had shifted to the next passenger.

Beside me was a woman named Collette, who seemed pleased that I was traveling to her country just to visit, not for business or to see family. The country was so beautiful and not enough people knew. I was Canadian? She had relatives in Ottawa, did I know them? She took my guidebook and, in a mix of French and English, pointed out places I must see. She produced a pen and marked most of the entries in the table of contents.

The seat-belt light came on, and we emerged from the clouds. Below us a coastline glittered with tiny lights. I had been warned not to do this, but of course it was too late now to turn back. When she asked if I had been to Lebanon before I shook my head.

The customs clerk at the Beirut airport eyed my passport and glanced up at me with disinterest. One hand thumped down with its stamp and the other waved me through.

A taxi took me into the city and left me at an inexpensive hotel, the Mace. Surprised that getting here had been so easy and unsure what to do now, I sat on the bed and turned on the television. A woman in clothes that left only her face and hands exposed smiled as she held a box up to the camera. English letters on the box read ALWAYS. After that commercial came the news, and there was the city I had left a few weeks before, Jerusalem, orange lights flashing on sheets draped over figures lying still in the street. At the bottom of the screen were Arabic words that I could now read: "Martyrdom operation in occupied Palestine." It was September 2002, two years and five months after the last night at the Pumpkin.

# 52

I WALKED AROUND downtown Beirut and found that it was possible at times to sense, like a barely detectible odor of cumin, the old cosmopolitan Middle East—the one where Jews, Armenians, Greeks, Europeans, Muslims of various types, and many others, mingled and did business with each other in an atmosphere of congenial corruption.

I sat one evening at the Temple of Jupiter in Baalbek as bats flapped around the Roman columns. I was ripped off in the soap markets of Tripoli. I took a cable car up to a giant white statue of Mary that looked over the Mediterranean, her hands away from her sides, palms facing forward. She was made by craftsmen from France more than a century ago, and her pose suggested she might be wondering where the French had gone and when they would be back to pick her up. I stood at her feet with the Maronite pilgrims, men with golden crosses in the Vs of their unbuttoned shirts and women observing the Levantine tradition of putting on your tightest miniskirt and scantiest blouse before heading off to touch the Virgin. We have our own equivalents. These experiences will not be unique to anyone who has visited Lebanon, something I urge you to do if you can—it's a country that deserves a better history than it has had and a better future than the one that seems in store.

One Sunday morning I joined a hiking group that left Beirut in a van for the hills to the east. When we arrived I inhaled the familiar black licorice scent of fennel, the smell of Galilee in the summer. We began picking our way along a high ridge. There were a dozen of us, all Lebanese except for two Frenchwomen and me. The guide warned us not to stray from the path because of Israeli cluster bomblets left over from the 1982 war and not to take pictures of the nearby military emplacement maintained by the Syrian army. On one of the slopes between us and the sea I saw an enormous cross that I took for a stark emblem of Christian faith before realizing it was the pillar of an off-season ski lift. After we had been walking for a while I realized that I had assumed the natural position of the sergeant at the back of the line.

I offered my bottle to a man and woman walking ahead of me, a third-grade teacher and a university student. They had come without water, and accepted it. The woman began to give me her list of places I must see, each of them the *most* beautiful. When I asked carefully about the south, she said, "No one goes down there. The Israelis could strike at any time." She had never been herself.

Upon discovering I was alone she pulled out a piece of paper and wrote down her email address. "I have friends all over the country," she said, "and you can stay with any of them." A girl with a bandanna tied over her hair was listening, and she wrote down her number on the same slip. On our way back to the city another of the hikers hosted us all at his villa for drinks. They were lovely, and I was very conscious of lying to them. When I made it to the hotel that evening I tore the paper into tiny pieces and threw them in the garbage.

# 53

On a Friday in one of the Shiite neighborhoods of Beirut I heard the mosques broadcast sermons over loudspeakers and found men sitting on curbs listening to sermons on car radios. I passed a damaged building that had no front wall, a remnant of the civil war, and saw ten poor men squatting there in the second-floor apartment, living their lives in view of the street. A few of them sat at the edge of what appeared to be a living room, their feet dangling over my head as I passed. There were no other Westerners in evidence.

The women wore black here, and the buildings were decorated with pictures of clerics. One of the most common posters showed the turbaned Hezbollah leader, Hassan Nasrallah, grinning as he brandished aloft a captured Israeli rifle with a green strap. I recognized the photograph—it was taken after the battle made famous by Ofer, the machine gunner who didn't get up. The rifle belonged to a guy who was shot several times that night but recovered and who I still meet sometimes around Jerusalem.

I came upon a huddle of men listening to a preacher's voice coming from a loudspeaker mounted on the roof of a taxi. Two adolescents in yellow Hezbollah jerseys stood nearby with a donation box shaped like the Dome of the Rock. My Arabic was good enough to understand that the sermon was about me; every few sentences I heard "Jews." There was a shopkeeper standing in his doorway nearby, and I was surprised when he gave me a friendly glance. Walking over and assuming my most Canadian demeanor I asked him what this was about. Nothing, he said, and he put his hand on my shoulder and actually pushed me away down the sidewalk. He stopped pushing only when he was sure I would keep going by myself. Don't worry, he said, it is nothing. He was still smiling.

I sat at a plastic table on the street downtown one evening and was joined by two guys in their twenties who grasped my hand, bought me a carrot juice, and welcomed me to Lebanon. Did I like it here?

"Lebanon is the best place on earth—paradise," the first one said, placing his hand on my arm for emphasis. He said both of them were trying to get visas for Europe. He waved by way of explanation at the driver of a moped parked at the curb. The driver, a delivery-man, waved back. He starts every day at 7 a.m. and finishes after 8 p.m., the first one said, and makes nothing.

A loudspeaker in a nearby mosque issued the call to evening prayers. "I love to hear that in the morning, when the streets are empty," the first one told me. They were both Shiites. I asked if he prayed, and he appeared surprised by the question. "Of course not," he said. "But I trust God, and I'm a good person." The second one nodded.

What did I think about the Middle East? Did I agree that America was bad? Canada, however, was good, very good. "And do you like Jews?" asked the first one, and I sipped my carrot juice, and said no I did not, not particularly.

"Jews are very bad," he said. "They kill little babies." He extended his forearms with his palms facing each other to show me how little. After we parted ways with friendly handshakes I went back to the dingy pension to which I had relocated to save money, two floors up from the Wash Me car wash. Near the reception desk sat a man with a faded T-shirt reading, in Arabic, THE LIBERATION OF THE SOUTH: A CELEBRATION FOR THE NATION.

# 54

IN THE NORTHERN part of Mount Lebanon, near the town best known as the birthplace of Khalil Gibran, I encountered eight people my age walking along the Qadisha River. One of them, in a baseball hat and track pants, stopped to ask if I was Lebanese. This was in English, so I suppose he already knew the answer. His said his name was George, and he was from one of the towns nearby. They were going down to the river to have a picnic and play some music, he said; another member of the group carried a guitar. Would I come?

We made our way down to a small clearing by the riverbank and settled down in a circle. One or two of them were lawyers, a few were university students, one was a nurse, and one, in flared jeans and a shirt that reached her midriff, was a teacher. They offered me a plastic cup of orange soda and a goat cheese sandwich. I liked them, all of them, at once. On leave from the army, when I still lived on the kibbutz on Mount Gilboa, I used to go with some of the kibbutz kids down to a spring in the valley with a guitar and a watermelon pilfered from the dining hall, and we would lounge around in the late afternoon enjoying the fact that we had nowhere else to be. It was the same sort of thing.

They wanted to know where was I staying, and when I said the name of the town—Bsharee—they hooted. Why would I stay there when the neighboring town of Ehden was superior in every way? This, I gathered, was where they were from.

"Ehden is more beautiful," said Emilio, a lawyer with slick hair. "And more modern," said George. "The people are nicer," said Shadi, whose curly black hair and glasses gave him the appearance of an eastern European intellectual of the 1930s. I read later that there had been bad blood between the two Christian towns since the civil war. The warlord family from Bsharee was allied with Israel and the rival family from Ehden with the Syrians, and one night in 1978 men from Bsharee went down the road to Ehden with guns, and among the dozens they killed was a son of the rival family, the Franjiehs, as well as his wife and daughter, who was three. One of the girls with us was a Franjieh. I pleaded ignorance and promised to stay there next time.

Three members of the group—the guitarist, his fiancée, and the teacher—were Muslims, George said, not from the Christian villages of the hill country but from the coastal city of Tripoli. "Our fathers fought each other," he said. "Everyone thought they were defending something." He shrugged. "To us it is not important."

"My brother married a Christian girl," said the guitarist. "We're breaking down the wall."

"Like Pink Floyd," said Shadi.

As a student of the Middle East, George asked, did I agree that Israel had engineered the American plan to invade Iraq so that the Palestinians could be transferred there?

I hadn't heard this interpretation before, but the sentiment was becoming familiar. I had many similar conversations in those weeks, and worse, and had already noticed the availability of the *Protocols of the Elders of Zion* and related literature in the better bookstores in Beirut. If I harbored an idea that in Lebanon I might meet some who were prepared to join me in a Middle Eastern version of the Christmas truce, when German and British soldiers left their trenches to meet each other for a game of soccer in no-man's land, or that I might at least detect a hint that such a thing was possible, it was not to be. I didn't find no-man's land.

The guitarist strummed a few chords and they sang a song everyone knew by Lebanon's beloved Fairuz. When the tempo picked up, Shadi hoisted me by the arm and led me in a clumsy but enthusiastic *dabka*, after which we sat down to applause and laughter. Then the guitarist's fiancée, who hadn't said much, began to sing and everyone fell silent. She wore a blue shirt and pink eye shadow, her voice was thin, her delivery mournful and unadorned. It was "The Story of Love," by Oum Kalthoum, the greatest Arab chanteuse of all.

Emilio leaned back next to me and observed her. "All of our songs are stories of love," he said. I have often thought of those eight and wondered where they are now.

# 55

And finally to the south.

It felt wrong to reach south Lebanon just by driving south in Lebanon—for us south Lebanon was a different universe with different rules, accessible to members of certain combat units through gates in our northern border. My last trip had been in a convoy of armored trucks. This time I was in a minivan taxi, Arabic pop on the radio, the sea a blue expanse out the window to my right.

The taxi was staffed by two men, one the driver, the other a barker with tattooed arms and a sun hat whose job was to draw customers and make change. As we barreled down the coastal road from Beirut in the sunshine the barker hung out the door shouting "Sidon, Tyre!" with glee at the people we passed. He seemed to be doing this mainly for his own entertainment, as the van was full. A child sat on her mother's lap and chewed the seat in front of her. The roadside villages grew more ragged as we drove, the women's dress more conservative, the yellow flags more numerous as we approached Hezbollah's territory in the former security zone. At the entrance to the city of Tyre we were greeted by the guerrilla group's patron saint, the ayatollah Khomeini, glaring from a poster next to a Kentucky Fried

Chicken franchise, which was full. Tyre was to be the base for my exploration of the south.

When the minivan stopped the barker pointed me toward a swarm of yellow cabs, one of which dropped me a few minutes later at a pension in the city's Christian Quarter. After I paid, the driver told me to be careful. Why, I asked. He motioned with his hand toward Israel and grinned.

The beach at Tyre is superb, with broad white sands and clear waters. I spent the evening drinking local beer at a shack run by a man named Walid, who wore only a pair of cutoff jeans. He spent a few years studying architecture in France, he told me, before he tired of Europe and came home. He had everything he needed here, he said. He played pool with a friend under a bare lightbulb.

I was a twenty-minute drive up the coast from my parents' home in northern Israel—or would have been were there not an impassable border in between. I had traveled twelve thousand miles to get here. The salty air was the same. In the weak light the border was visible to the south, the same ridge visible from my parents' rooftop, ending in its promontory of white chalk extending into the sea. But now I was on the wrong side.

# 56

I WALKED INTO a grocery store to buy something to drink, and found two men sitting among shelves stocked with dry goods. They were surprised to see a tourist, because there was no good reason for any to come to this town. The proprietor stood up and greeted me. I was Canadian? That was very good. In fact he had cousins in Ottawa, did I know them? I bought a raspberry Popsicle. The second man seemed to have a job that is an important staple in many Middle Eastern businesses, that of the friend or relative who sits around your shop doing nothing. Welcome to Nabatieh, he pronounced, and I thanked him. He wanted to know if I had heard of someone named Hassan Kamel al-Sabbah, and looked disappointed when I said I had not.

Hassan Kamel al-Sabbah, the proprietor repeated. I shook my head.

From Nabatieh, he said. He invented—he searched for a word—the electricity.

The light, the second man said.

Back on the street a man passed me with a metal jug of coffee in one hand. In the other were glasses that he clinked together in an elaborate rhythm. He stared at me. Other people stared at me. I was pushing my luck.

I stopped at a bakery, and the owner took my elbow, led me to a table, and brought me a plate of sticky pastries. When I was done he undercharged me. Welcome to Nabatieh, he said as I left. Farther down the street I noticed a large sign on a traffic island, a portrait of a man in a traditional Arab headdress. He was not one of the usual Shiite clerics or teenage Hezbollah martyrs whose portraits were everywhere. The Arabic letters underneath the man's face read HASSAN KAMEL AL-SABBAH.

This al-Sabbah was, I later learned, an inventor who did important work for General Electric on circuitry and solar cells before he was killed in a car accident near Elizabethtown, New York, in 1935. He was a different kind of local hero, perhaps, for those so inclined.

To the east was a row of hills, the ones I was looking for. There were buildings in the way, so I walked until I had a clear field of vision and could make out an artificial protrusion on the ridge under an overcast sky. It was the Pumpkin. I was getting closer.

I wanted to find the places we saw from the outpost, the ones we all knew by heart: the villas, the Cal-Tex gas station, the al-Ghandour hospital, the Monastery of Saint Anthony. I began walking through the town in the direction of the hill. Soon what life there had been on the streets began to thin.

Now I was among shops cluttered with old car parts. I passed a vendor selling charcoal. Men gave me unfriendly looks from dilapidated storefronts, but no one stopped me. I passed a group of middle-aged men standing next to a row of parked taxis and saw that they were laughing. They were laughing at me. They stopped when

I walked over, and each of them shook my hand. I was Canadian? Canada was good.

Journalist? one asked. Tourist, I said, and if they were surprised they didn't show it.

One of them took my camera and photographed me with the other drivers. My back was to the hill, and I could feel it behind me. I wondered what they would do if they knew. A driver with a bushy gray mustache asked me to help him move to Canada. I said that Canada was so cold and Lebanon so beautiful—why would he want to leave? He placed his hand on my shoulder and spoke as if he had prepared a statement. "Lebanon is the most precious gift of God, the most precious thing he gave us," he said, and then waved his hand at the dismal street. "But here there is no way to change your life." I wrote that down as soon as I found a quiet place to open my notebook, because I didn't want to forget exactly how he said it.

I was now being carried along by the magnetic pull of the outpost. There were no more sidewalks in this part of town, just garages and Hezbollah signs. The wall of one building was covered in portraits of martyrs from the war against us. I turned left into a neighborhood that spilled off the road and stretched toward the foot of our hill. There was nearly no one around, and I knew the farther I walked the flimsier my excuses for being here would become.

An old man was sitting on a chair outside a store, holding a cane and looking at me through thick glasses. Two little boys played on the ground next to him. What was I looking for, he asked in English. I told him I was a Canadian student and that I liked to see regular neighborhoods and not tourist sites.

Was I alone, he asked, and I said yes. He suggested that I be careful—it was dangerous to walk around alone. When he asked if I liked Nabatieh I said I did, though I didn't and wanted badly to leave. Could we once have thought, even in jest, that coming back here one day would be a happy reunion with a place we knew well? There seemed no happiness in this rough town, certainly none that would be available to me.

"Things are getting better here," he said, "since they left." He pointed to the protrusion on the hill. I asked him how it was when *they* were here, not saying "Israelis," as if by pronouncing that word it might be clear to him who I was. He looked at me as if he pitied my ignorance. "Bad," he said. "Very bad. But I wasn't here. I was in Gabon, in Africa." I asked him if it was really dangerous to walk around. "It was a joke," he said, but he didn't smile.

I followed the dirt shoulder of the road into the neighborhood closest to the hill. A man passed me in a grimy yellow baseball hat with a Hezbollah logo, pushing a wheelbarrow. Now I was at the edge of the town. Beyond me was the dead zone leading to the beginning of the slope. Above me was the outpost, just a half mile away but inaccessible from down here in the valley; I knew it could be reached only from the eastern side of the ridge, on the old army access road, and getting there would be a separate trip. Now it was possible to imagine what it meant to have the horizontal slit of the lookout post peering down at you always like a malevolent eye.

I came to a two-story building surrounded by a low stone wall. A white sign was affixed to an electricity pole, and I am not sure why I was so surprised that it read DIR MAR ANTONIUS—the Monastery of Saint Anthony. Perhaps until then I was still not convinced that the line between my life and the life of this town could ever truly be crossed. One week during our second tour someone fired rockets at us every evening from behind this wall.

On the road ahead I saw a row of familiar villas, some of them no longer abandoned and others under construction. If I may try to explain what this felt like, imagine growing up with a painting of a forest on the wall of your room, a picture that you see every day and that is intimately familiar, and waking up one morning under the trees. I walked no farther and left the town as quickly as I could.

# 57

In the morning I set off from Tyre in a battered cab unencumbered by seat belts and headed inland into the old security zone. This was the most important part of the journey, and I felt something of what a mountain climber must feel leaving camp in unpredictable weather for an attempt at the summit.

I had considered engaging a tour guide to show me around southern Lebanon but abandoned the idea when I realized someone like that would be inclined to ask questions. Instead I hired a taxi driver named Ibrahim. We agreed on a price for two days of exploration. On the first I would visit only sites that a tourist would know from the Lebanon guidebooks and in this way gauge his level of suspicion. On the second, I would try to reach the hill. I could still think of no reason that anyone but an Israeli soldier would know where the Pumpkin was or want to go, and knew that the moment I directed him there would be the most fraught of the trip.

Under Ibrahim's dark mustache his front teeth were missing. On his dashboard was a photograph of a round toddler, his son. We didn't talk much, as he knew only a few English words and I was concealing my own minimal Arabic to avoid blurting out Hebrew by mistake, a fear that accompanied me throughout my time in Lebanon. The old cab's engine showed unexpected spirit, and Ibrahim wrenched the steering wheel to the left every time someone in front of us moved too slowly for his liking, passed in the opposite lane and then twisted the wheel rightward again to avoid oncoming traffic. He must have seen my expression—I was considering the irony of surviving south Lebanon as a soldier only to meet my end there on the grille of a cucumber truck—because he patted my leg and said, "No problem."

At the main intersection of one dusty village I saw a wooden mock-up of the Dome of the Rock with a Hezbollah flag and the English words JERUSALEM, WE ARE ON THE WAY.

We drove along the border fence and drew abreast of a frontier post inside Israel. I recognized it as one named after a kind of orchid. Ibrahim slowed, pointed and said, "Israel," pronouncing it *ees-ra-eel.* I assumed there were soldiers in a concrete lookout emplacement at that moment peering through binoculars at a yellow cab inside Lebanon that had slowed down, which it should not have done, making out a driver with a mustache and someone in the passenger's seat. I knew what the post looked like inside: a low ceiling, a horizontal opening facing Lebanon, an electric kettle, radio equipment with a few frequencies babbling, packages of processed cheese. Ibrahim pointed his index finger in the direction of the base, thumb up, mimed a gunshot, and then sped away.

We passed through Shiite towns bedecked with Hezbollah flags and posters of martyrs and leaders. After a while it seemed to me that Hezbollah's artists might have become bored painting the same Hassan Nasrallahs and Ayatollah Khomeinis, and I started noticing the same portraits but with backgrounds of airbrushed neon colors, the kind of style you might have seen on the side of a van in America in the 1970s. I saw one Nasrallah with a pop-art background of comic book dots and imagined a frustrated artist laboring in a basement covered in his own unsold paintings, churning out another portrait of the leader to cover rent.

When we stopped to buy gas the attendant was surprised to see a tourist. He pumped my hand and asked me how I liked Lebanon. I told him I loved it. Across the street was a Hezbollah flag and a mock battery of twenty rockets aimed at my family.

We stopped at the abandoned UN compound at Kana, where a sign read THE NEW HOLOCAUST: 18 APRIL 1996. Inside the base were signs of the impact of our munitions: shards of glass, blackened earth, shrapnel-pocked walls, twisted metal, and pulverized concrete. In one empty room were three little boys playing with pieces of junk. When a detachment of Israeli spotters became pinned down by a Hezbollah battery set up near the compound, our artillery fired to cover their retreat and hit the compound instead, killing more than a hundred ordinary people who thought they were safe inside. There were long marble sarcophagi and a few photographs, each with a name and date of birth. One smiling young man was born the same year I was, 1977.

# 58

I PLANNED OUR route for the next day knowing it would take us past the intersection that led up to the Pumpkin. But I still didn't know how to explain why I wanted to go up the hill.

Traveling along the border again that last morning we stopped at the old gate once known as the Good Fence, through which Lebanese villagers used to cross into Israel for work and medical treatment in the days of the security zone. There were Israeli soldiers in a small fortified position a few yards away on the other side, and I worried that someone might recognize me. Israel is so small that this wasn't impossible. I pulled my baseball hat lower.

A Hezbollah sign in Arabic and English recounted a suicide attack in 1988, one of many such signs around southern Lebanon documenting operations against the Israelis. I was taking a picture of the sign when from the corner of my eye I saw a man exit a small building and stride toward me. His beard was neatly trimmed, he was dressed meticulously in black, and his demeanor indicated that he was in charge. Would I have guessed a few years earlier that in my first close encounter with a Hezbollah man I would be armed only with a camera and notebook? He shook my hand, but his gaze remained suspicious.

When he asked, in Arabic, if I was a journalist Ibrahim answered for me: He's a tourist from Canada. Welcome, the man said, still cold, and motioned for me to put the camera away. I signaled in response that this was no problem. We shook hands again, but he didn't smile or move. I got back in the cab.

When we were down the road Ibrahim turned to me, gestured toward the man, and said, "*Muqawama*." Resistance. I nodded, but Ibrahim didn't seem satisfied. "Hezbollah," he said, and I made sure to look more impressed this time.

# 59

WE CLIMBED INTO Khiam and, after some navigation through narrow streets, reached the Hezbollah museum located on the edge of town. The museum was in the old prison from the years of the security zone, the one run by the South Lebanon Army and our own secret services.

I'm not sure how Khiam Prison would compare to Hezbollah's hostage basements, which have yet to be opened to tourists. But it was a foul place even with the jailers gone. Inside were bare cells and a small exercise yard, and when I looked up I saw the sky divided into squares by strands of barbed wire. The Hezbollah curators had affixed signs in Arabic and English next to doorways; one was labeled ROOM FOR THE BOSS OF WHIPPERS. Some of the graffiti left by visitors on the walls was in English: "Jews are AIDS," "Jews are a cancer to society," "Kill all Jews," and so forth. The Christians who staffed the prison seemed to be off the hook.

With us were two busloads of visitors from Bahrain and Saudi Arabia, the men in khakis and carrying video cameras, the women draped in black. We all filed into a small theater to watch a movie that included reenactments of methods of torture. One showed a man being whipped as he lay facedown on the floor with his feet up on a chair. There were a few children in the theater, and one little boy began to scream; his mother tried to calm him in vain, but she didn't take him out. The film ended with footage from the liberation of the prison on the morning after the Pumpkin and the other outposts were destroyed, after the Shiites of the south realized the Israelis were gone, that their own fighters had won: crowds running toward the compound, shouts of *God is great!*, gaunt bearded men reunited with jubilant families. I felt happy for them.

From the prison we descended to the Litani River and picked up the old convoy route. We soon came, as I knew we would, to the little restaurant on the riverbank, the one we used to see from the trucks. It felt as if I had an old reservation. The restaurant was exactly as I remembered it—a ramshackle awning and a few tables. We sat down near the water and the proprietor, a woman with her hair modestly covered, came over. Her two sons were there, Musa and Hassan, and another youth named Issa. There was enough room for my whole platoon, but Ibrahim and I were their only customers.

In our dream of returning one day we would sit in this restaurant, unafraid, and watch the river. In the dream this meal was perfect. But my fish was overcooked and dry, and we were beset by flies. So it is with the realization of dreams. I was so moved to be in that place that it didn't matter.

When we finished I took out my wallet. "How much," Ibrahim asked in Arabic.

"Fifteen dollars," replied Issa, in Arabic.

"Twenty-five dollars," the proprietor translated into English, and I paid. Of course the question of who was tricking whom was not as clear as she thought, and the meal was worth more to me than any other I have eaten, before or since.

Once over the bridge we began climbing west up the Ali Taher range. On the roadside was another Hezbollah sign, this one with a photograph of a young man with a broad smile. He wasn't solemn or sad like most martyrs. He looked like a person it would be nice to meet. He also seemed to be trying to grow a beard with patchy results. The English text on the sign was titled MARTYR BILAL AKHRAS'S AMBUSH DEFYING THE ZIONIST ARROGANCE.

> At dawn on June 10, 1996, the arrogance of the Zionist army was dealt a painful blow near the strategic "Dabshe" outpost which had been meant by the occupation to be one of the symbols of that arrogance. An Islamic Resistance squad penetrated the Zionist security wall and set a dexterous ambush for a Zionist 15-strong foot patrol.
>
> When the patrol was in the fire range and as it approached the ambush spot, the Resistance men peppered it with a shower of rocket propelled grenades and machine gun fire killing or wounding the fifteen enemy troops.
>
> The close range confrontation turned into a direct encounter carried out by Resistance man "Bilal Akhras" who was martyred during the operation as he advanced toward the patrol troops, inflicting more casualties in their ranks.

"Dabshe" was the Arabic name for our hill. There were thirteen men, not fifteen, in the Israeli squad. But it was otherwise an accurate description of the Falcon Incident, from Avi's time at the Pumpkin, in which five soldiers died and the rest were wounded. Yaacov, the new soldier, saw a running figure but hesitated to shoot, and the sergeant fired and killed him instead. That was Bilal. I have a photograph taken the following morning, given to me by one of the medics. It shows Bilal in forest-green fatigues, sprawled crooked-limbed on his back among some bushes.

# 60

THE INTERSECTION APPEARED as I knew it would—a right turn onto a road cutting upward toward one of the peaks at forty-five degrees. This was where a few of us crouched on our first day in Lebanon, gun sights trained on two men who turned out to be looking not for us but for game.

The turn was unmarked, as I assumed it would be, and there was no way a first-time visitor would know what was up that road. I had come all the way back here for this, but if I said anything Ibrahim would know I had been there before. I had no idea who he was or whom he might tell. My courage failed. I said nothing, and the turn leading to the Pumpkin receded behind us.

I conducted a furious argument with myself, the intersection growing more distant with every second. I changed my mind and asked Ibrahim to stop the car.

I touched the camera around my neck and said I wanted to go up to the top of the hill we had just passed. I want to take pictures, I said, and there must be a nice view up there. I knew it was implausible. Ibrahim looked unhappy. I reached into my wallet and found a twenty-dollar bill. "For the gas," I said, and put the bill in his hand

and closed his fingers around it. He put the car in reverse and drove backward all the way to the intersection.

When I was a child the Royal Ontario Museum had a dark hallway lined with dioramas illustrating the life of prehistoric man, life-sized figures wearing skins, cooking mammoth meat, fashioning arrowheads. I saw something similar now as we drove up the hill. In the vegetation to our left I saw us checking the route for bombs, my friends spread through the brush, sweating through our uniforms in the heat. The dog was out in front and behind it the sturdy shape of Harel, foot raised in midstride.

We reached the bend in the road where a soldier once mishandled a machine gun and fired a burst into the asphalt beside me. I remembered the silence after that happened, the way we looked at each other. I knew the boulders along the road. I had searched the ground for trip wires dozens of times. I struggled to pretend I had never seen any of it before and suspect I was doing a poor job, but in the driver's seat beside me Ibrahim didn't seem to notice or care. I did my best to look surprised when a jumble of concrete finally came into view at the top of the hill. "Israel radar," Ibrahim was saying, but in my ears was shouting in Hebrew—*Run*—and the rumble of trucks. He stopped the cab in the convoy yard and switched off the engine. Everything was still.

When my feet touched the ground I found myself looking out over a river valley leading toward a brown-sloped massif; it was the end of a long summer and the hills were dry, their colors dun. It was still beautiful.

I left Ibrahim to think whatever he was thinking and proceeded alone. I didn't run. On concrete slabs I saw Hebrew graffiti, as unlikely now as hieroglyphics. One read, "Aryeh, we want invitations to the wedding." At the outpost's entrance I saw a black car parked beside the gate. It was empty. I saw no one at all, and there was no answer when I called out. So preoccupied was I in those moments with the realization that I had actually returned that the odd presence of this car receded. I walked past it into the Pumpkin.

Inside the embankments were enormous concrete pieces and twisted metal rods, the remnants of the roof brought down on the last night. I sat on one of the blocks. There was a familiar smell of dust and baking cement which I had forgotten. The outpost was always alive with soldiers laughing, cursing, or shouting, the clanking of tanks, radio static. The hill had been crowded and energetic, but the people who animated it were gone, and it felt dead.

Atop the western embankment a Hezbollah flag flew at last, but it was just a ragged scrap of fabric that had once been yellow. For a time this hill was worth our lives, but even the enemy seemed to know that now it was worth nothing at all. That seems like a universal lesson for a soldier, knowledge available if you are lucky enough to get through your trials unscathed and able to make it back afterward to whatever hill you were once told to capture or defend—and if you are willing to listen to what these places try to tell you about the insignificance of your decisions, about the way you were borne this way and that by tides beyond your comprehension.

It was late in the day, but the stillness made it seem like Readiness with Dawn again, a pause for heightened attention. Be quiet, look around. Listen. Who is here with you?

I was alone.

Are you ready?

There was nothing to be ready for. History had left this spot and moved on.

Where are you? I was on a hilltop in the Middle East, a place on the periphery of the periphery, a parched hill like thousands of others, a good vantage point from which to look at the world. In the years that have passed since I stood on the rubble that day I have been trying to understand what I saw. What I grasp changes with time, but two lessons are clear.

When I went back to the Pumpkin in the fall of 2002 I thought it was a conclusion—an end to that war, and to the disquiet it left me and the others it touched. But I sensed then, and know now, that I was wrong. It wasn't a conclusion. On the hill we had been at the start of something: of a new era in which conflict surges, shifts, or fades but doesn't end, in which the most you can hope for is not peace, or the arrival of a better age, but only to remain safe as long as possible. None of us could have foreseen how the region would be seized by its own violence—the way Syria, a short drive from the outpost, would be devoured, and Iraq, and Libya, and Yemen, and much of the Islamic world around us. The outpost was the beginning. Its end was still the beginning. My return as a civilian was still the beginning. The present day might still be the beginning. The Pumpkin is gone, but nothing is over.

When I scrambled up to the top of the embankment I found the trench sunlit and undamaged, the floor covered in toppled sandbags of tan and burgundy. Some were my own handiwork. I walked above the trench, exposed. This was something we could never do in daylight, and because old instincts had reappeared I had to keep telling myself not to jump down to safety. It took no time to remember the view. I might have been on guard duty that morning.

Looking north I saw the slope where Mordechai was wounded in his tank and Lior killed. Farther to the north were the ruins of Red Pepper.

I walked along the rim of the trench until I stood by one of the posts abandoned by its sentry in the Pumpkin Incident of 1994, near the spot on the floor beneath the parapet where a soldier lay that day on his back, still warm. Today he would be forty-one.

From there I could see south toward the Forest, where the bomb crippled our vehicle on the night Natalie got undressed; where I once crouched and saw our missiles float toward the town; where the engineers were surprised and cut down near the Falcon Bend.

Under the embankments, the entrance blocked by rubble, were the old sleeping quarters, dark rooms that might now remain sealed for centuries. If, in the future, someone goes to the trouble of uncovering the doorway, they might see faint Hebrew scribbling on the walls, or pick up an ancient cigarette carton. But they won't know the lives of the people who once rolled bleary from bunks inside and went to do what others asked, and who sometimes did not return.

From where I stood atop the outpost I saw that with no one to tend to the hilltop, nature was taking it back. You would like everything to stop, to acknowledge that the disappearance of human beings matters, but of course nothing stops. There is a song about that in Hebrew, written by a woman from a kibbutz that lost eleven men in the war of 1973. She repeats the words "but the wheat is growing again," because she can't seem to believe that's possible.

The trench was filling up with the contents of disintegrating sandbags. Vegetation sprouted between concrete slabs. We have a list of hills that will exist forever in our shared memory. The Pumpkin will never be one of them.

I passed the guard post where Eran, the altruist, was hit by a rocket. He is still an altruist.

Weeds grew around the gun emplacements where Avi once looked at the hills of Lebanon, as green in the rainy season as the ones awaiting him in Donegal or Cork.

Upon returning to these events years later I found myself drawn in the evenings, after a day of writing or interviews, not to literature from my own country or era but instead to the poems and reminiscences of men like Edmund Blunden and Isaac Rosenberg from the Great War of a century ago. They had been torn from normal existence and dispatched to the very edge of life, beyond the edge—

I, too, have dropped off Fear—
Behind the barrage, dead as my platoon,
And sailed my spirit surging light and clear
Past the entanglement where hopes lay strewn

That's Wilfred Owen. The church bells in his town were ringing to announce the armistice when his parents' doorbell rang and a telegram informed them of his death. I wasn't sure at first why these writers had my attention now. This was all in the distant past, and my experiences did not compare with theirs. It was, I realized, their perception, so much clearer than mine, of the thinness of the line between here and gone. This is the second lesson the Pumpkin taught me, and still is teaching me—how flimsy is the border between those two states, between Avi and me. This is the debt I owe that place, and the reason I am grateful for my time there.

I happened to be lucky on the hill, and so remained convinced of my invincibility, of the impregnable nature of the line. Only now do I understand it's just an angle, a moment, a clerk's stamp on a piece of paper, a step in one direction or another. This belated insight provoked an unexpected feeling that pursued me throughout the writing of this book. The feeling was retroactive fear. My twin sons are seven and my daughter three. Sometimes when the boys are wedged on either side of me, listening to a story, or when I'm pushing the little one on the swings in the afternoon and she points the tips of her red sandals at the top of the cypress trees, I know I could have missed this. I almost missed it. Others did.

I continued along the outpost's western embankment, a warm wind beginning to pick up. It was then that I saw a shape move outside the trench a few yards away.

The shape was the back of a young woman's head. Her hair was dark and sleek. My first thought was that there couldn't be a woman at the Pumpkin—that was one of the inviolable laws of the place. But there she was, seated on the outer slope of the embankment near where the flag had once been planted, facing away from me and toward the town spread beneath us on the plateau.

She hadn't noticed me, and I stood still. I'm not sure I could have moved had I wanted to. I heard a murmur coming from her direction, but it was too deep to be hers. It belonged to a man. Then her head dipped down and out of my line of vision, and the murmuring stopped. Only after a few seconds of silence did I understand who and what had finally taken the hill.

The cab was waiting in the old convoy yard. The Pumpkin receded through the rear window, and I knew I wouldn't see it again.

# NOTES ON SOURCES

Quotes that appear in the text in quotation marks are from documents, recorded interviews, or my own notes. Dialogue retrieved from memory appears without quotation marks.

All military documents and newspaper articles cited in the source notes are originally in Hebrew, translations mine.

## Chapters 1–3
Descriptions of Fighting Pioneer Youth (Hebrew: Nachal, an acronym for Noar Halutzi Lohem) basic training in 1994 are from conversations in 2013 and 2014 with members of Avi's platoon, drafted into the brigade's engineering company in March 1994: Matan Dishon, Gal Perlmutter, Ilya (Elia) Libman, Amit Nisim, Amos Squverer, and Dotan (Guli) Wolfson. Additional details are from a booklet of photographs and writing compiled by the platoon after their discharge in 1997 and from my own experiences as a recruit at the same base three years later. Avi's childhood stories are from interviews with Yossi and Raya Ofner in 2013 and 2014.

## Chapter 4
"A. reached basic training": Courtesy of the Ofner family, translation mine.

## Chapter 5
"Bent double, like old beggars under sacks": Wilfred Owen, "Dulce et Decorum Est," written 1917, revised 1918. In *Wilfred Owen: The War Poems*, ed. Jon Stallworthy (London: Chatto & Windus, 1994).

The list of books that Avi borrowed from the library is glimpsed on a computer screen in a film made by the Ofner family, *Kahalom Ya'uf* (Like a flitting dream), during an interview with Naomi Bassi, the librarian from the kibbutz (Sde Eliyahu) where Avi attended high school. The lullaby is Emmanuel Harussi's *"Shkav Beni"* (Lie down, my son) (1929).

Biographical information about Romain Gary is from David Bellos, *Romain Gary: A Tall Tale* (London: Harvill Secker, 2010). Gary's *The Kites* (French: *Les cerfs-volants*) was published in French by Editions Gallimard in 1980 and appeared in Hebrew in 1983 as *Afifonim*, published by Am Oved. At the time of this writing a first English translation has been undertaken by Miranda Richmond-Mouillot for the U.S. publisher New Directions.

### Chapter 6

From interviews with Avi's platoon. Gal Perlmutter's nickname in Hebrew was "the Good Fairy," but I have rendered it "the Angel" because that roughly matches the Hebrew meaning without the connotations attached to *fairy* in English.

"actively trained, like the French Army, for the war of 1914": Romain Gary's memoir *Promise at Dawn* (New York: Harper & Brothers, 1961).

### Chapter 7

For background on the 1982 invasion, see Ze'ev Schiff and Ehud Yaari, *Israel's Lebanon War* (New York: Simon & Schuster, 1984). For background on the security zone in Hebrew, see Moshe (Chico) Tamir's memoir *Milhama Lelo Ot* (Undeclared war) (Tel Aviv: Israel Defense Ministry Publishing, 2005). See also the first chapter of Avi Issacharoff and Amos Harel's *Korei Akavish* (Spider's web) (Tel Aviv: Yediot Books, 2008), about the Lebanon war of 2006, translated into English as *34 Days: Israel, Hezbollah, and the War in Lebanon* (New York: Palgrave Macmillan, 2008); and Gal Luft, "Israel's Security Zone in Lebanon—A Tragedy?" *Middle East Quarterly* 7, no. 3 (September 2000): 13–20.

"born with a knife in their hearts": Haim Gouri, *"Yerusha"* (Heritage), in the collection *Shoshanat Ruchot* (Windrose) (Tel Aviv: Ha-Kibbutz Ha-Meuhad, 1960).

The relay of bonfire signals "from the Mount of Olives to Sartaba" is from the Mishnah (Rosh Hashanah, ch. 2).

Outpost Pumpkin (Hebrew: Mutzav Dla'at) was built by a company of reservist engineers in the summer of 1983, according to interviews I conducted in 2013 with documentary filmmaker David Kerpel, a member of the company. No importance seems to have been attached to the event: I could find no photographs or official record, and when I contacted a second soldier from the company and the battalion commander neither remembered the outpost from a distance of thirty years.

## Chapter 8

Ilya is Ilya (Elia) Libman, interviewed in 2014.

## Chapter 9

Eran is Eran Stern of the Givati Brigade Engineering Company. The description of the Pumpkin Incident of October 29, 1994, is from interviews in 2013 with Eran; with the outpost commander, Maor Binyamini (then deputy company commander); and with Ofir Zilberstein, then a sergeant in the company. Additional information comes from a redacted two-page account of the incident in the Israel Defense Forces (IDF) archive, titled "Appendix 1: Attack on Outpost Pumpkin 29/10/94," compiled by Division 91 HQ, November 7, 1994. The Hezbollah video can be found on Youtube: https://www.youtube.com/watch?v=lMuaiDcFp8A.

"though he was physically unharmed he never recovered": Chen Kotas-Bar, "Eighteen Years Later: The Soldier Who Abandoned His Post Talks about the Shame," *Maariv*, July 28, 2012.

The soldier killed at the outpost was Sgt. Almog Klein, twenty-one. The officer whose back was bloodied was Lt. Moshe Gerstner, and the soldier with him was Ofir Zilberstein. Eight years later, in April 2002, as a twenty-nine-year-old officer in the reserves, Gerstner was killed in fighting with Palestinian gunmen in the West Bank city of Jenin.

The Hezbollah account is from the Arabic book by Salim Elias, *Al-Muqawama al-Islamiyya wal-Amal al-Askari* (The Islamic resistance and military operations) (Beirut: Lebanese Cultural Center for Printing, Publishing, Translation, and Distribution, 2006). Translated for me by Dr. Dan Naor.

"Disgrace" was the one-word headline of a page 2 article in *Yediot Ahronot*, October 31, 1994.

"When fear and crying become respectable subjects": Ron Ben-Yishai, "All They Needed to Do Was Look Up," *Yediot Ahronot*, November 4, 1994. Ben-Yishai writes in the same article that the role of parents in the army is becoming "like the parent-teacher association."

The incident in which a soldier punched a rude motorist in the face was witnessed by Ofir Zilberstein, interviewed in 2013.

## Chapter 10

"A Bank, Not a Tank": Headline of a front-page analysis piece on October 31, 1994, in the daily *Maariv*.

"The fighting spirit has been broken": Yaron London, "The Givati Symptom," *Yediot Ahronot*, November 1, 1994.

## Chapter 11

From an interview with Yohai Ben-Yishai in 2014, shortly after his retirement from military service, and from interviews with Avi's parents and the members of his platoon. The precise date of the incident in Arnoun in late 1994 is unclear; I found no record of it in the IDF archive. Avi's surprise at being tired by the sprint for a stretcher is from an interview with Matan Dishon.

## Chapter 12

From interviews with Yossi and Raya Ofner, and with members of Avi's platoon.

## Chapter 13

"Morning will rise soon here in Lebanon": Letter to Smadar Oren, October 7, 1995. All letters courtesy of the Ofner family. Additional details from an interview with Smadar Oren, 2013.

One of the medics who treated Yohai Ben-Yishai was Omri Levi, interviewed in 2013.

## Chapter 14

"lost a rifleman and two trackers in an ambush among nearby olive trees": This incident occurred on June 18, 1995. The three were Staff Sgt. Hillel Rosner of the Givati Brigade Engineering Company, and trackers First Sgt. Hani Muhammad and First Sgt. Hashem Rahal.

The quotes from Rabbi Yehuda Leib Ashlag (1885–1954) are from his essays "The Giving of the Torah" (1933) and "Critique of Marxism in light of new reality, and a solution to the question of the unification of all streams of the nation" (mid-1930s, precise publication date unknown). I used the Hebrew versions archived on the website www.ohrhasulam.org, run by followers of Ashlag in Israel. Translations are mine.

Descriptions of the May 17, 1995, incident in which Eran Stern was wounded and Staff Sgt. Amir Kra, the lookout, was killed, are from interviews with Eran in 2013; with Helena Kurz Kra, Amir's mother, in 2014; and with Avishai Sofer, a comrade of Amir's who was at the outpost during the incident, also in 2014. Additional information from a redacted document in the IDF archive titled "Incident at 'Pumpkin' May 17, 1995." The TV footage, including raw footage shot that day, was provided to me by Eran Stern, whose family obtained it from the TV station after he was wounded. The conversation between Amir Kra and the woman soldier at headquarters in Israel, Daniella Raz, appeared in a television segment prepared in 2013 by Channel 1 reporter Yair Weinreb, a friend of Amir's. Raz (now Raz-Weinreb) later became Weinreb's wife, and he presented the conversation as she remembered it. I spoke with Weinreb in 2013. Amir's note ("In a few days I'll be on my way to another outpost . . ."), on three pages from a yellow notepad, dated December 1994, was provided to me by Helen Kurz Kra.

## Chapter 15

"to calm my internal combustion": Letter from Avi to Smadar, May 29, 1996.

"Now I'm keeping it in hiding" and "The point is that we are changing": Letter from Avi to Smadar, May 28, 1996.

"I understood, only too well, those who refused to follow de Gaulle": Gary's *Promise at Dawn.*

## Chapter 16

"Not many journalists come here": Sever Plocker, "Two Fingers from Nabatieh," *Yediot Ahronot*, April 3, 1996.

Avi's travel plans and thoughts on Ireland ("a country of contradictions, just like me") are from a letter to Smadar, May 29, 1996. In the letter he mentions that U2's "One" came on the radio and he stopped writing to listen.

## Chapter 17

The "friendly fire" incident mentioned involved a Golani Brigade platoon near the Lebanese town of Taibeh on December 30, 1998. The soldier killed was Staff Sgt. Ohad Zach, nineteen.

The description of the Falcon Incident (Hebrew: Irua Baz) of June 10, 1996, is from interviews with Yaacov Artom in 2014; from an account of the battle written by Yaacov after his discharge; from a file in the IDF archive titled "'Falcon' Ambush—Engagement by Engineering Company with Hezbollah Cell in the Sector of Outpost 'Pumpkin,'" dated June 26, 1996; and from a longer file on the incident prepared for use as an educational tool for soldiers, titled "Ali Taher Range Incident." The medic who remembered treating the wounded but could not remember hearing any sound is Amit Nisim, interviewed in 2014. The soldiers killed were Lt. Yishai Shechter, twenty-one; Lt. Lior Ramon, twenty; Staff Sgt. Eshel (Amir) Ben-Moshe, twenty-one; Staff Sgt. Idan Gavriel, nineteen; and Sgt. Yaniv Roimi, twenty.

"Everything's okay": Interview with Yossi and Raya Ofner, 2013.

## Chapter 18

"I have the feeling that everything is disintegrating": Letter to Smadar, June 11, 1996.

"His discovery of danger does not come at once": Lord Moran, *The Anatomy of Courage* (London: Eyre & Spottiswoode, 1945), quoted in Peter

Vansittart's *Voices from the Great War* (Harmondsworth: Penguin Books, 1983).

"short, bloody, spasmodic silent fights": Gary's *Promise at Dawn*.


## Chapter 19

Details on Avi's time in Tel Aviv are from interviews with Yossi and Raya Ofner, and from a scrapbook prepared by his roommates, Rotem and Orit (no last names appear), and given to the Ofners in February 1997. The scrapbook includes a letter from the roommates describing the time they spent with Avi, as well as notes they exchanged with him in late 1996 and early 1997.


## Chapter 20

"bought for $15 at stores selling garden ornaments": Interview in 1999 with Sheikh Nabil Qaouk, Hezbollah's head of military operations, quoted in Judith Palmer Harik, *Hezbollah: The Changing Face of Terrorism* (London: I.B. Tauris, 2004).

Details of Avi's last days at the Pumpkin are from interviews in 2013 and 2014 with Yossi and Raya Ofner, Gal Perlmutter, and Mordechai Etzion.


## Chapter 21

Details of Avi's arrival at the airstrip on February 4, 1997, are from interviews with Yossi and Raya Ofner, and in 2013 with Yair Barkat (Bareket), then commander of the Pumpkin (and at the time of the interview a senior officer in the IDF's Home Front Command). Barkat recalled the argument with Lt. Col. Moshe Mualem, the commander at the airstrip, who died in the crash.

Details on the helicopter accident are from the IDF archive, "Commission of Inquiry into the Circumstances of the Yas'ur Accident of February 4, '97," April 16, 1997. (*Yas'ur* is the Hebrew designation for the Sikorsky CH-53 transport helicopter.) This report was declassified by the archive for the first time at my request, though not in full. It concluded that the possibility of a technical malfunction, or the detonation of explosives on board, was "low," and that the accident was most likely the result of pilot error.

Some additional details are from a January 2011, report on the crash compiled for the army by military historian Meir Amitai ("The *Nachal* Brigade in the Helicopter Disaster, February 4, 1997").

Harel, the soldier who had departed for officers' training, is Harel Kaufman, later my commander in the brigade's antitank company. The other ten members of his team, led by Lt. Dotan Cohen, twenty-two, were on the Helicopter headed to Beaufort Castle. The trackers Hussein and Kamel are Master Sgt. Hussein Bashir, thirty-five, and Sgt. First Class Kamel Rahal, twenty-six, both from Beit Zarzir. Gil is Lt. Gil Eisen, twenty-one. Shiloh is Staff Sgt. Shiloh Levi, twenty-two. Avner is Staff Sgt. Avner Alter, twenty-two; the description of Avner's reaction to the Falcon Incident comes from a letter he wrote to his girlfriend (dated November 21, 1996), included in a memorial book which can be found in the library at his kibbutz, Ashdot Yaakov. Tom is Staff Sgt. Tom Kitain, twenty-one, of the Jewish Arab village Neveh Shalom / Wahat es-Salaam, near Jerusalem. Abukassis is Lt. Shai Avekassis (a Hebraicized version of Abukassis), twenty-two. Vitaly is Sgt. Vitaly Pesachov, twenty-two; information on his birthplace is from the Defense Ministry's website, www.izkor.gov.il. Mulatu is Sgt. Mulatu (Asher) Gideon, twenty-one; information on his family's trek from Ethiopia is from press reports published after the crash. Vadim is Capt. Vadim Melnik, thirty-four; information on his life is from a memorial book compiled by his family, found in the memorial archive for victims of the helicopter crash, Har Ve-Gai high school, Kibbutz Dafna. For more on the victims, see www.the73.org.

Information on the contents of Avi's pack and where it was recovered—not at the site where his helicopter crashed but rather beneath the point where the two Helicopters collided—as well as the fact that his body was found not in the wreckage of the helicopter but some distance away, is from Yossi and Raya Ofner. At least a dozen soldiers (seventeen, according to Yigal Mosko, writing in *Yediot Ahronot* on January 30, 1998) were thrown from Helicopter 903 before it crashed, most of them landing in and around the backyard of the Gershoni family of She'ar Yeshuv. Weeks later imprints of several bodies were still visible in their yard, including that of one soldier clearly carrying a rifle; Avi's parents were informed that Avi was the only soldier found carrying a rifle, hence the assumption that this was him. Additional information on the helicopter accident is from interviews in 2013 with Ruth and Amnon Schreibman, parents of Lt. Nir Shreibman, who was twenty when he died in the crash; with Eli Ben-Shem, chairman of the memorial organization Yad Lebanim and father of Lt. Kobi Ben-Shem, who was twenty-one; and with Yoram Alper, father of Staff Sgt. Idan Alper, twenty-one. The testimony of the watchman is from the IDF's official report on the crash. His name was redacted in the version provided to me, but Meir Amitai identifies him as Khalil Sa'id of the Druze town of Ghajar.

Photograph courtesy of the Ofner family. The soldier in the center is unidentified; on the left is Amit Nisim. Date unknown, probably 1995 or 1996.

## Chapter 22

The soldier who remembered being taken to identify the bodies in Tel Aviv is Omri Levi, interviewed in 2013.

## Chapter 23

Details on Avner Alter, including his appreciation for the song "Children of Winter '73," are from the memorial book compiled by his family and found in the Ashdot Yaakov library. Bruria is Bruria Sharon, currently the librarian at Kibbutz Ashdot Yaakov and keeper of the Four Mothers archive, interviewed in 2013.

## Chapter 24

Eran Shachar, "Mothers in the Service of the Military," *Ha-Kibbutz*, March 6, 1997.

## Chapter 25

The description of life on the hill in the weeks after the crash is from interviews with Mordechai Etzion in 2002, 2003, and 2014; with Matan Guggenheim (then a soldier in the engineering company, now a filmmaker) in 2013; and with members of Avi's platoon in 2014. Descriptions of Mordechai's battle on February 27, 1997, are from my interviews with him; with Yair Barkat (Bareket), the outpost commander at the time; and with Gal Perlmutter, one of the medics. Additional information is drawn from documents in the IDF archive and from my own memory of seeing the video filmed from the lookout post that night. Lior is Sgt. Lior Shabtai, nineteen.

## Chapter 26

Jonah is Jonah Mandel, interviewed in 2014. The Alterman fragments are from *Kochavim Bachutz* (Stars outside) (Tel Aviv: Yachdav, 1938). Translations are mine.

## Chapter 27

The article introducing the Four Mothers ("The Home Front Takes the Offensive") was by Eran Shachar, *Ha-Kibbutz*, April 3, 1997. The four women featured were Ronit Nachmias, Miri Sela, Yafa Arbel, and Rachel Ben-Dror.

## Chapter 28

The officer killed on September 7, 1997, by a mortar shell at the Pumpkin was Lt. Avraham (Avi) Book, twenty-two. The officer and radioman from the engineering company killed (on June 25, 1998) by a Hezbollah explosive after the unit was moved from the Pumpkin were Lt. Amit Asouline, twenty-one, and Sgt. Or Cohen, twenty.

## Chapter 29

The battle in which twelve members of a naval commando squad died took place near Ansariya, Lebanon, on September 4–5, 1997. The brush fire in the Saluki riverbed, which killed five soldiers, was on August 28, 1997. Orna is Orna Shimoni, interviewed in 2013. Lt. Eyal Shimoni, twenty-one, was killed on September 18, 1997.

## Chapter 30

From interviews with Orna Shimoni.

    The attack at the Pumpkin that wounded two tank crewmen, including

Alexei Yermenko, who lost both legs, took place on December 26, 1998 (IDF archive document 115-1210/2003). One of the soldiers sent to retrieve the crewman's legs was Oriel Benzvi, interviewed in 2013.

### Chapters 31–32
From my own memories and notes.

### Chapter 33
Information on the military experiences of my maternal great-grandfathers, Thomas Dodd and Archie Affleck, in World War I, and of my grandfather Hugh Affleck in World War II, is from historical research conducted by my uncle, CWO (rtd.) Colin Affleck.

### Chapter 34
"The voice of the Lord": Psalm 29:5. "With me from Lebanon, my bride": Song of Songs 4:8.

### Chapter 35
The description of the incident is from my own memories and notes, with additional detail from interviews in 2013 with other members of my platoon: Adam Yadid, Yoni Yakiri, and Nadav Strizover.

Be'eri Hazak's poem "Lord of the Universe" appears in *Bivchi Oti Tiktzor* (In Tears Shall You Reap Me), a collection of his poems and letters published by his family after his death (Hakibbutz Hameuchad Publishing, 1974). Translation mine.

### Chapter 36
From my own memories and notes.

### Chapter 37
Information on residents of the security zone, including the size of the population, is from Plocker, "Two Fingers from Nabatieh." The commander at

Beaufort Castle who tried to speak the local language was Yiftah Guy, later a school principal, interviewed in 2013.

## Chapter 38
From my own memories and notes.

## Chapter 39
From interviews in 2013 with Bruria Sharon and Orna Shimoni. Information on the Ofer Sharon affair is from interviews with Bruria Sharon and documents provided by Bruria; from press reports; and from an interview with another soldier present at the battle, Elad Lerer, in 2013. The interview with Ofer Sharon ("Why I Didn't Get Up") was conducted by *Haaretz* reporter Avichai Beker and published on October 7, 1999. Three officers died at Qalat Jabur: Lt. David Granit, twenty-two; Lt. Liraz Tito, twenty-one; and Maj. Eitan Belachsan, thirty.

The song "Ammunition Hill" (*"Givat Hatachmoshet"*) was written in 1967 by Yoram Taharlev. Eitan, the machine gunner mentioned in the song, is Pvt. Eitan Naveh, twenty-three when he died on June 6, 1967.

## Chapter 40
From my own memories and notes.

## Chapter 41
On Hezbollah rebuffing Israeli attempts to negotiate a withdrawal, see the deputy Hezbollah secretary-general Naim Qassem's *Hizbullah: The Story from Within* (London: Saqi Books, 2010), 228, and also Palmer-Harik's *Hezbollah: The Changing Face of Terrorism*, 134.

"Syria's foreign minister declared that doing so without Syria's consent would be an act of war": Farouk a-Shara, "Reactions to Government Decision," *Yediot Ahronot*, March 6, 2000. On March 12 a-Shara was again quoted in *Yediot Ahronot* condemning the Israeli withdrawal plan, calling it a "trap" and saying, "Israel can't disconnect itself from Lebanon without the permission of Beirut and Damascus."

The Ali Taher battalion commander who saw the Four Mothers as meddlers, and later changed his mind as an educator, is Yiftah Guy, interviewed in 2013. The senior commander who called them the "four rags" in February 2000 and then met with them to apologize (as reported in *Yediot Ahronot*, February 20, 2000) was Shmuel Zakai, commander of the Golani Brigade. Brig. Gen. Erez Gerstein's comments on the Four Mothers were published in *Yediot Ahronot* on June 9, 1998. On February 28, 1999, a Hezbollah bomb destroyed the vehicle in which Gerstein was riding with two soldiers (Sgt. Maj. Imad Abu Rish, thirty-five, and Staff. Sgt. Omer El-Kabetz, twenty-two) and the radio reporter Ilan Ro'eh, thirty-two; all four were killed.

## Chapter 42
From my own memories and notes.

## Chapter 43
"king anointed with salt, crowned in wreaths of seaweed": Meir Ariel's 1993 song *"Zirei Kayitz"* (Seeds of summer), on the album of the same name.

Makov is Eran Makov, interviewed in 2013 (as deputy commander of the army division in charge of the West Bank). Vasily Grossman's "In the Town of Berdichev" appears in the collection *The Road*, trans. Robert and Elizabeth Chandler with Olga Mukovnikova (New York: New York Review Books, 2010). The incident in which Amstel was apparently killed took place on February 6, 2000, as reported the following day in "The Medic Raced to the Wounded—and Was Killed," *Yediot Ahronot*, and then in greater detail in the same paper on February 9, 2000 ("Four-Legged Heroes"). The medic who was killed was Staff Sgt. Yedidya Gefen, twenty. Amstel's handler, who was wounded, was Ro'i Ben-Lulu.

## Chapter 44
Blutreich is Ofer Blutreich, interviewed in 2013. Kahana is Ran Kahana, interviewed in 2013 as a brigade commander in the West Bank. Additional information on the last days at the Pumpkin is from interviews in 2013 with Daniel Uman, then a platoon commander, and Ori Asoline, then a

logistics sergeant. The last soldier to die at the Pumpkin was Sgt. Amir Meir, nineteen, killed on February 8, 2000, when an antitank rocket hit his guard post. The last soldier to die inside the security zone was Sgt. Tzahi Itach, nineteen, killed when an antitank rocket hit his guard post at Beaufort Castle on February 11, 2000.

"No One Wants to Be the Last One Killed in Lebanon": Eitan Glickman, *Yediot Ahronot*, February 10, 2000.

"The soldiers entering Lebanon project a sense of dejection": Nahum Barnea, "The Shadow of Lebanon," *Yediot Ahronot*, weekend magazine, February 11, 2000.

## Chapter 45

Additional details on the withdrawal are from Tamir's *Milhama Lelo Ot* (Undeclared war); from Yigal Sarna, "The Crew of Tank 3 Shuts the Door on Lebanon," *Yediot Ahronot*, June 2, 2000; from another description of the withdrawal in Eitan Glickman, Amir Rappaport, and Doron Golan, "6:40 a.m.: The Last Soldier Leaves, the Gate Is Locked," *Yediot Ahronot*, May 25, 2000; and from a long article by Ron Ben Yishai, "The Lebanon Withdrawal: The Real Story," *Yediot Ahronot*, September 29, 2000.

## Chapter 46

From my own memories and notes.

## Chapter 47

"this war will be forgotten in a few years": Tamir, *Milhama Lelo Ot* (Undeclared war).

## Chapter 48

"a light at the end of the Palestinian tunnel": Naim Qassem, *Hizbullah: The Story from Within.*

The border attack in which Hezbollah guerrillas took the bodies of three soldiers took place on October 7, 2000. The cross-border infiltration at Kibbutz Matzuva, in which six Israelis were killed, took place on March 12, 2002. The two army technicians were shot while on a border antenna on July 20, 2004. The suicide attack at the Sbarro pizzeria took place on August 9, 2001. The attack at the Dolphinarium club in Tel Aviv was on June 1, 2001. Lt. Daniel Mandel, twenty-four, was killed in Nablus on April 15, 2004.

"Hezbollah . . . was the 'A-team'": Max Boot, *Invisible Armies: An Epic History of Guerrilla Warfare from Ancient Times to the Present* (New York: Liveright Publishing, 2013).

**Chapter 49-53**
From my own memories and notes.

**Chapter 54**
The names that appear here are pseudonyms. No other details have been changed.

**Chapter 55–59**
From my own memories and notes.

**Chapter 60**
The song *"Ha-chita tzomachat shuv"* (The wheat grows again) was written in 1974 by Dorit Zameret of Kibbutz Beit Hashita.

"I, too, have dropped off Fear": From "Apologia Pro Poemate Meo," in *Wilfred Owen: The War Poems.*

**Additional interviews (conducted in 2013 unless otherwise specified)**
Matan Barak, soldier in Fighting Pioneer Youth Antitank Company wounded at Beaufort in 1997; Nitzan Gavriel, medic, Fighting Pioneer Youth Engineering Company; Lior Lifshits, commander of Ali Taher sector 1997–99; Yossi (Yossifoon) Kauffman, Armored Corps crewman at the Pumpkin in mid-1990s and unofficial outpost historian, interviewed in 2012 and 2013; Eran

Niv, Fighting Pioneer Youth Antitank Company commander 1997–98, at time of interview commander of the army officer school Bahad 1; Simchi Rubin, Givati Brigade soldier at the Pumpkin, early 1990s; Moshe (Chico) Tamir, expert on guerrilla warfare and commander in Lebanon, author of *Milhama Lelo Ot* (Undeclared war); Amir Tzuberi, Golani Brigade soldier at the Pumpkin, early 1990s; Elisha (Lulu) Yekutiel, a childhood friend of Avi's.

# ACKNOWLEDGMENTS

I would like to thank Amy Gash, my editor at Algonquin Books of Chapel Hill, and the staff at Algonquin; my agent Deborah Harris; and my agent Judy Heiblum of Sterling Lord Literistic. For help with research: Yossi and Raya Ofner, who were beyond generous with their time and the material they have kept since Avi's death in 1997; Yifat Arnon and Iris Sardas at the archives of the Israel Defense Forces (IDF) at Tel Hashomer; the members of the IDF spokesman's unit; Mohammed Odeh of the Commonwealth War Graves Commission; and all of the many people mentioned in the text and source notes who shared their memories with me. For reading different iterations of the manuscript and offering advice: George Eltman; Mitch Ginsburg; Tali Griffel; Aliza Raz-Meltzer; Sharon Ashley; Stephanie Saldana; and Fleming Kress, whom I was lucky to have teach me creative writing in high school and who had superb writing suggestions twenty years later. Special thanks to my mother, Imogene Friedman; my sister, Sarah Sorek; and my father, Raphael Friedman, without whom this book would not have been written. And thanks most of all to my wife, Naama, and to our children, Michael, Aviv, and Tamar.

The writing of this book was enabled by the Sami Rohr Prize, created by Sami Rohr's children in honor of a great lover of books in general and Jewish books in particular. I would like to think that Sami (1926–2012) would have found this book worthwhile; I am, in any case, forever in his debt and that of his family.

*Pumpkinflowers* is dedicated to Avi Ofner and the others who chose in those years to defend our country in the Lebanon security zone and who died doing so. May their memory be a blessing.